The Image of God

Give Man His Dignity

Augustine Kelechi Ikegwu, O.SS.T.

En Route Books and Media, LLC
St. Louis, MO

En Route Books and Media, LLC
5705 Rhodes Avenue
St. Louis, MO 63109

Cover credit: Sebastian Mahfood

Copyright © 2021 Augustine Kelechi Ikegwu, O.SS.T.

ISBN-13: 978-1-952464-79-9
Library of Congress Control Number: 2021938526

Imprimi Potest granted by,
Reverend Father, (Bro.) Alban Martial EBE ZOGO,
Order of the Most Holy Trinity and of the captives,
(The Vicar; Vicariate of St Agnes)
November 9, 2019.

No part of this book may be reproduced, stored in a retrieval system, or transmitted in any form, or by any means, electronic, mechanical, photocopying, or otherwise, without the prior written permission of the authors.

Dedication

I dedicate this book to the Most Holy Trinity.

Contents

Acknowledgments i
Foreword v
Preface vii
Abstract xiii

Chapter 1: Introduction 1
    Early Thought 4
    The Thought of Mirandola 5
    Modern Perspective 6

Chapter 2: The Image of God 11

Chapter 3: Aspects of Human Dignity 19
    The Differences Among Humans That Touch Upon Human Dignity 22
        Race 22
        Skin Color 28
        Sex 30
        Age 32
        Education 37
    Concomitants of Human Dignity 38
        Right to Life 38

Liberty and Pursuit of Happiness............................40

Chapter 4: Abuses of Human Dignity and the Human
    Person..43
    Threats to life...44
        Abortion 44
        Genocide...48
        Human Sacrifice 54
        Indiscriminate Police and Military Attacks............60
    Threats to Liberty..63
        Slavery...63
        Human Trafficking 66
        Kidnapping..70

Chapter 5: The Respect for the Dignity of People................73

Chapter 6: Instrumentalization and Dehumanization
    of Man 79

Chapter 7: Practices that Violate Human Dignity 87
    Social Exclusion...88
    Torture 91
    Rape 95
    Absolute Poverty...96
    Labor Exploitation..101
    Bonded Labor 105

Chapter 8: Different Stages in the Development of the Idea
    of Human Dignity...109
    Cosmo-centric View..110
    Christo-centric View...114
    Logo-centric View...116
    Polis-centric View..121

Chapter 9: The Church's Stand on Human Dignity..........125

Chapter 10: Africa: Human Dignity at Risk.......................147
    The Colonization of Africa..151
    Tribalism..160
    Life..163
    Racism in Africa..168

Chapter 11: Man with Dignity and the Society..................177

Chapter 12: Conclusion..187

Acknowledgments

In acknowledging, man manifests a sense of oneness and association with another as destined by God. He who appreciates the other recognizes the humanness, dignity, and image of the invisible God in him. On this backdrop, I consider it an obligation to appreciate the below listed individuals.

All thanks to the Most Holy Trinity, the creator of mankind, for inspiring this redemptive work through this humble servant. The coming to fruition of this work will only occur according to the will of Him Who is infinite in Love and mercy, He who desires that this book becomes an instrument of liberation to His people from all yoke of captivity.

I owe a debt of sincere gratitude to my general minister Rev. Fr. (Bro.) Luigi Gino Bucarello, O.SS.T, provincial minister Rev. Fr. (Bro.) Giovanni Martire Savina, O.SS.T, together with the community minister, Rev. Fr. (Bro.) John Uzoma Odemenam, O.SS.T., and other team of formators such as: Rev. Fr. (Bro.) Jean Constant Nganga Silaho, O.SS.T, Rev. Fr. (Bro.) Baviel Mbila, O.SS.T., and Rev. Fr. (Bro.) Jospin Bouetoumoussa, O.SS.T.

This appreciation remains incomplete without mentioning the Vicar of his Vicariate (Saint Agnes), RT. Rev. Fr. (Bro.) Alban Martial EBE ZOGO, O.SS.T., who gave the nod of approval for the publication of this work, all for the greater glory of the most Holy Trinity.

A debt of gratitude is assigned to the editors of this work: Gloria Ogo, author of *While Men Slept*, Anthony J. Dixon; Allan J. Smith (KSC), author and editor of *The Cries of Jesus From the Cross*; Isabel Smith (LSC); Chad Newton (Ph.D.), a scholar in Qualitative and Exegetical Analysis, and to Sir Stephen Michael Leininger whose professional formatting enhanced the final form of this manuscript.

To forget one's family is to forget one's existence. Without reserve, I ascribe tremendous thanks to my parents, Nze (Mr.) Damian A. Ikegwu and Lolo (Mrs.) Martina N. Ikegwu, my brothers, sisters, especially Ernest, Joseph, Queenderline, Joy, Adenike, Jennifer, Christopher, James, and John Ikegwu together with Obinna and Chinwendu, for their priceless advice, encouragement, and contributions. May the good Lord reward them all.

In the words of Ralph Waldo Emerson, "The ornament of a house is the friends who frequent it."[1] On the above

---

[1] Ralph Waldo Emerson, *Domestic Life, Society and Solitude*, American essayist, lecturer, poet (1870), available online at https://blog.coldwellbanker.com/the-ornament-of-a-house-is-the-friends-who-frequent-it.

Acknowledgments

podium, I say thanks to Chief Hon. Mrs. Deborah Chinwe Okah, Chief Lady Theresa Anukwa, Mike Aquilina Ph.D., Dennis McGeehan, Brent Dean Robbins, Ph.D., Chidinma S. Ikea, Ph.D., William Hemsworth M.Div., MATS, Paul A. Nelson, Gaby Bustos, Mrs. Angelina Okere, Hon. Dr. Okwu Ejike (TOE) Ekechi, Mr. and Mrs. Casimir Mounkala, Prof. Boniface Okere, Sir Mighty Nkwocha, Bar. Pauly Okere, Comrade Umunnakwe Michael, Bro. Francis Ikechi Nwaorgu, Bro. Francy Edvy-Carel Mounkala O.SS.T, Bro. Nnadi JudeFelix Chetachukwu MMT, Bro. Peter Anugwolu CRS, Rev. Fr. Ibe Gasper, RT. Rev. Msgr. Anthony Uwakwe, Rev. Fr. Henry Ogbuji, Rev. Fr. Joseph Don Ybanez Castro CRS, Rev. Fr. Malachy Eleanya C.SS.P, and Rev. Sr. Rachael Consolata Ngumo C.SS.T, for their encouragement, support, advice, and prayers, which provided enlightenment and encouragement on the journey of writing this work.

Foreword

Just as Africans, who occupy the content of this book, are beset by problems of varying capacity, the young author of this work, currently based outside the shores of Nigeria, encountered great difficulties in the course of his research.

Though a Nigerian whose principal English language is backed by his native Igbo language and familiarity with Latin, his formation studies took him to French-speaking countries for the most of last year where he was immersed in French language and was restricted mainly to French-language literature. Likewise, his access to the Internet was severely limited. These factors, compounded by a personal adaptation to French culture, proved a challenge in preparing this work though I attempted to smoothen some of those difficulties through limited and very occasional communication.

Being a Nigerian, the author has had a box seat from which to observe the trials of his people. Not content with mere observation, he waded into the maelstrom, considering that his life has been greatly affected by adverse forces working upon the people, from school years to family life, and the trials peculiar to religious and tertiary studies. He is currently still outside his home country of Nigeria.

The resulting work is an honest and heartfelt analysis of a tragic situation with a keen, rational conclusion indicating what needs to be done and how the issues it identifies might be approached. All these make the work ideal for Catholics and students in particular.

ANTHONY J. DIXON

Preface

Though *The Image of God: Give Man His Dignity* concentrates primarily on Africa, its content is relevant globally. In this work, the African man is portrayed as a victim of inter-religious and socio-political conflicts, causing a loss of his dignity both as a human and as a member of the African community.

In Nigeria, a country of mixed religions, there exist frequent inter-religious conflicts which not only claim lives, but also affect the nation's socio-political and religious lifestyle. Around 2008 and 2009, during my secondary school years, I came in contact with world history and the African continent in particular. It was during that period I discovered that Nigeria wasn't the only country whose citizens were dehumanized, degraded, and robbed of their dignity, especially as this tragedy unfolded in other continents as well.

In 2013, a four-year philosophy program at the University facilitated my personal studies and research on the African continent. My adult experiences on global killings, criminality and dehumanization, especially in African societies both present and past, evoked my quest for liberation and reform in Africa, all the while calling to mind God's distinctive call, "come let us make man in our own image and likeness" (Gn 1:26).

From infancy till today's date, man is to me the beauty of all creatures based on the dignity accorded him and God's image present in him. Catholicism–my faith–respects man, his life and dignity, and teaches against instrumentalization and dehumanization of human persons as discussed in this book.

Years of personal experience collaborated with extensive research and tossed me into a reflective state of mind, including thoughts on how to carry out the mission of liberation. Despite my vocation to serve in the Lord's vineyard, I always pondered on how to involve myself with humanitarian groups. I did not consider writing down the many problems facing an African man and possible solutions to them.

Arriving in Brazzaville at the beginning of February in 2018 to face my vocation felt like the end of my aspiration. However, early in the second half of the same year, the flame rekindled. Primarily, this was due to the charism of the family into which God called me; it resonated with what I had nurtured all these years.

The motivation to put this research into writing came from the advice of friends which, on the 10th of March 2018, birthed the title of this book.

The formation of the second half of this title *The Image of God: Give Man His Dignity* is coined from an in-depth study of the title *The Image of God*, a theological affirmation of man's existence as created by God in his own image and likeness, thus existing as a being with great dignity. It highlighted the preciousness of the human as a person, his life, and existence in human societies. Without the first part of the title, the book would be devoid of foundation, for man came from God. The second part, *Give Man His Dignity*, covers the societal forces and acts of man's inhumanity in the African society. Also, it calls upon man's consciousness towards the life and dignity of another through fraternal love, which binds us as one family and as equals in Him who created us.

The Image of God: Give Man His Dignity analytically evaluates the origin and existence of man as a dignified being in the society. This touches the threefold aspects of a man's life in the African context, the social, political, and religious aspect.

In this work, the African man is called to a sober reflection about himself in relation to others: the reason for and meaning of his existence on earth–as a being made for others while he also makes his way back to God. In his relationship with other men, he is expected to manifest his dignified nature. Hence, this work argues for the necessity of a positive relationship between members of African societies despite religious, social, and political differences, as this enables man to co-exist and collaborate with others as willed by his creator.

The dignity of man is the Divine Origin he possesses. It defines the worth of man and marks his uniqueness as the superior being within all of God's physical creation. His preciousness is ascribed to the power of his rationality, his free will and ability to love. Any action contrary to this state of man dehumanizes and objectifies him.

Man as a societal being is seen by the Catholic Church as a religious being. Through her teachings, which defend the personhood and dignity of man, a solid defense of my writing can be presented affirming the importance of religion in the human society, expressing an interior attitude that calls the attention of the African man towards the vitality of others through fraternal love. This love equalizes and mirrors the image of God in him.

The Image of God: Give Man His Dignity requires a deep reflection of one's self before the individual can actualize this great call of love. This book is an easy read that calls us to a deeper journey within ourselves, a journey that will hopefully enable us to put into practice the teachings contained herein—and *Give Man His Dignity*.

It also serves as a guide for those who wish to live fully in human society. Students in the departments of Humanities and Religious Studies will glean it as sound research. For the dehumanized, through analysis expended in this work, it becomes an aid to the liberation from captivity, justice for the condemned, an aid to the sick, a hope to the dying, and a call for attention to those treated without regard in the African societies.

Amongst numerous challenges encountered in writing this book, three were dominant. The first being a switch to a new language due to my religious formation in French-speaking countries. Working on new vocabularies and adaptation to a new culture slowed the tempo of writing of this book. Another setback was the limitation to internet access due to my Novitiate studies. Likewise, the availability of some beneficial materials and resources only in the French language during a one-year program in the Novitiate posed a hurdle.

Consequentially, it took seventeen months for this work, *The Image of God: Give Man His Dignity*, to transform from a thought into a book.

Augustine Kelechi Ikegwu, O.SS.T.

Abstract

The focus of this work is the African society richly diverse in every respect, save one: the common humanity of every African, whether rich or poor, young or old, male or female. This relates to those oppressed, dehumanized, and instrumentalized (viewed as a tool instead of a human created in the image and likeness of God).

This book examines the concept of human dignity and argues against the violation of that dignity and its concomitants. Violations have been known to occur through violence, political action, imposition of disadvantage, cultural and social prejudice, with the inclusion of stereotypes. This writing hopes to promote a society where humans will enjoy equal recognition through the law eradicating attitudes of superiority and inferiority. I also intend to posit that man deserves concern, respect, and consideration as a member of the African society and ought to be assured of his fundamental liberty.

Violation of human dignity reduces man to the status of a means to a state-determined end. These explorations of the substance of man's dignity and its implication have kept recurring in different generations and epochs and have produced arguments amongst intellectuals in various fields, including philosophers, psychologists, and ethicists, even within and outside the Church. This violation of the dignity and personhood of man is commonplace in many African societies. Thus, man is reduced to a non-rational animal, disregarding that he is created as an Imago Dei. The duty to respect and protect human dignity over-rides making any human a mere object of state policy. Such treatment of any man is an attack on the God-given value inherent in his being.

Chapter One

Introduction

The phrase *human dignity* is of recent origin, but the concept is as old as the sacred Scripture. Judeo-Christian Scriptures reveal that man is made *in the image and likeness of God*. Since God is the ultimate being, this creature made in His image deserves the ultimate dignity accorded to any created person or creation. In Psalm 8:5, man is made a little lower than God, his dignity is next to that of God but equal for all humans.

Amongst the Church and the Spanish and Portuguese explorers and colonizers, the term 'man's dignity' became controversial in the early sixteenth century. The *problem* stemmed from the discovery of American Indians, especially those of interest to Spain and Portugal. The Church embarked on an extensive missionary effort in South America, trailing in the wake of the Spanish and Portuguese explorers and colonizers. Colonizers, alongside their royal and commercial superiors, viewed these *new* people as less than human and, therefore, available as potential slaves to the new commercial enterprises. Meanwhile, the Church opined that these people were made in the image and likeness of God and should be considered free men entitled to liberty, property, and most importantly, baptism. Thus, they proposed considering these Indians as non-potential slaves.

Unfortunately, those on the path to justify the enslavement of the Indians artfully crafted arguments. They held that since God had not permitted the Church to know these Indians until now, the Indians were not included within the scope of *the great commission*. According to them, these Indians were sub-human, had no soul, and were not entitled to conversion and baptism. On this stance that they were not fully human and were lacking the image of God in them, they were free for enslavement.

The Dominican Bartolome de Las Casas joined Archbishop Juan de Zumarraga and the Bishop of Puebla Julian Garces in a meeting in Mexico in 1537. Their deliberations centered on opposing the would-be enslavers, and their arguments were conveyed to Pope Paul III.

Bartolome, the Spanish Dominican from the School of Salamanca, insisted that the American Indians were free men, who were genuinely made *in the image and likeness of God*. In his view, these American Indians had immortal souls in need of salvation and were within the scope of the Church's *great commission* to bring them to Christ. He insisted they were not to be enslaved as they were not enemies of Christ's Church in any sense.

Bartolome's arguments persuaded Pope Paul III, who issued the encyclical *Sublimis Deus* in 1537. It forbade the enslavement of not only the American Indians, but of all other innocent people; it was a strongly worded document stating that American Indians were humans possessing immortal souls and urged their evangelization. The encyclical forbade their enslavement and the enslavement of any new people not yet discovered, declaring them entitled to their liberty and right to property. *Sublimis Deus* also declared any contrary opinion to be the work of Satan. The papal encyclical was accompanied by an executing brief entitled *Pastorale Officium*.

Though the Spanish King, Charles V, had banned enslavement in 1530, the Decree of the King was annulled in 1537. The Spanish king requested that Pope Paul III withdraw *Pastorale Officium*, which he did, though the encyclical continued to have significant moral influence.

At Valladolid in Spain in the years 1551 and 1552, a formal debate ensued to resolve this matter of enslavement which posed a fundamental moral issue. Though Bartolome presented a persuasive argument, no conclusion was reached. This failed effort further exposed a need to clarify what had previously been accepted as part of the Christian teaching.

Slavery is a part of human history that emerged from the defeat of enemy combatants without limitation or concentration on skin color, race, or nationality. A defeated ally of some prince, king, or city was liable to enslavement by the victor, either for use or for sale. This was practiced throughout Europe, the Middle East, Africa, Asia, and America almost from the beginning of human existence.

The advent of Mohammedanism introduced religious identity as a factor in enslavement. Mohammedans enslaved Christian captives as *infidels*–for Mohammedanism was warlike from its beginnings. In response, the Church permitted that enemies of Christ's Church could be enslaved.

Early Thought

In Cicero's work, *De Officiis* 6, 106 (written in 44 B.C.), only a single mention of human dignity is observed where he wrote, "we see that sensual pleasure is quite unworthy of human dignity."[1] Here, he believed that man's higher intelligence required him to remain superior to other creatures.

Boethius, the Roman statesman and philosopher who wrote in the 6th century, defined human as "an individual

---

[1] M. Tullius Cicero, *De Officiis*, Book1: Moral Goodness. With an English translation. Walter Miller. Cambridge. (Harvard University press; Cambrigdge, Mass., London, England. 1913.) Sec. 106. available at http://www.perseus.tufts.edu/hopper/text?doc=Cic.%20Off.%201&lang=original and http://data.perseus.org/texts/urn:cts:latinLit:phi0474.phi055.

substance of a rational nature."² It is not a specific reference to human dignity, but rationality establishes a platform from which it can be considered.

More than 700 years later, Saint Thomas Aquinas, though happy with Boethius's definition, felt it should be further developed. He held that man is endowed with the powers of intellect, choice, and self-movement. These powers have as their ultimate goal the final fulfillment of our union with God. In this union is the perfection of man's dignity.

The Thought of Mirandola

The dignity of man remained a topic for consideration in Europe. Some forty years (give or take) earlier than the Spanish and Portuguese, Pico Della Mirandola, an Italian scholar and philosopher, composed the *Oration on the Dignity of Man* in 1486. However, it was not published until about two years after his death in 1494. In his book, Mirandola portrayed man as created by God to appreciate the rest of creation. Man, through exercise of free-will and intellect, possessed the ability to ascend the chain of creation even toward the hierarchy of Angels. The goal of

---

² Boethius, *A Treatise Against Eutyches and Nestorius, The Theological Tractates*, translated by Stewart, H.F. (London: Heinemann, 1918), 85.

this ascent was man's eternal union with God. Mirandola saw man's dignity as centered on the belief that only man could effect this change in himself whereas other creatures achieved change through external forces playing on them.

Modern Perspective

A lot of modern scholars are at a disadvantage in regards the concept of human dignity. In most cases, lacking a foundation in sacred Scripture and detached from any considerations of Church history, they know by mere intuition that human dignity is a useful and essential concept. However, they cannot find in their limited experience a base for it. Professor of Law, Linda Hawthorne, who, in the context of the Law of South Africa, wrote: "The recent pre-eminence of human dignity can be viewed as a reaction against the politics of the past, but is, in essence, a reflection of the fact that human dignity is the most important human right from which all other fundamental rights derive their existence."[3] Note that human dignity is not a *right*, but an innate human characteristic, and thus her choice of words, "all other fundamental human rights deriving their existence from it" can be characterized as wrong. Even as far

---

[3] Hawthorne, Linda, constitution and contract: Human Dignity, the Theory of Capabilities and Existenzgrundlage in (South Africa,SUBB Jurisprudentia 2011), 27.

back as 1776, members of the second Continental Congress in America declared: "We hold these truths to be self-evident, that all men are created equal, that they are endowed by their Creator with certain unalienable rights, that among these are life, liberty and the pursuit of happiness."[4] The source of our human rights is God ... not the benevolence of man's laws!

What are our human rights? Attempting to answer this question is like trying to hit a moving target. In the quest to create heaven on earth, lawmakers multiplied the numbers of human rights recognized in law. The concept of human rights gradually expanded until it reached insane proportions. For instance, in some American universities, *safe spaces* have been created in which students are insulated from thought or comment contrary to their beliefs or that may invoke uncomfortable feelings.

This book will dig beyond man's origin, his human dignity, and the origin of his rights. It will investigate aspects of human nature that affect our and other's human dignity, such as (but not limited to) race, skin color, sex, age, and education. It will study how human dignity in-

---

[4] Thomas Jefferson, "The Declaration of Independence," Historic American Documents, Lit2Go Edition, (1776), accessed March 19, 2020, available at https://etc.usf.edu/lit2go/133/historic-american-documents/4957/the-declaration-of-independence/

fluences human behavior and perceptions. Further, it will tackle the concomitants of human dignity, including the right to life, liberty, and the pursuit of happiness.

The scope of this work will examine abuses of human dignity and threats to the right to life including abortion, genocide, human sacrifice, indiscriminate policing, and military attacks. Discussion will cover threats to human liberty including slavery, human trafficking, and kidnapping.

The influence of others' beliefs towards human dignity and how it affects the inter-relationship among individuals will not be left out. Since one person's liberty ends where it collides with that of another, we will examine the instrumentalization and dehumanization of humans. When an individual is seen as a means to an end, the result is a disregard for his dignity. This is often justified by appeals to the *greater good* of the society as in the case of Socialism, including, but not limited to, National Socialism (Nazism), Communism, and Fascism. These ideologies have trampled human dignity underfoot and have led to the death of millions of people. Those fortunate enough to escape death were subjected to every conceivable abuse and abrogation of their rights. All of this was spawned by the thought of Karl Marx, whose poisonous influence is subtly at work today around the globe.

Not exempted from this work is the examination of other violations of human dignity, including torture, rape, absolute poverty, corruption, restriction of initiative, and labor exploitation.

To adequately produce an overview of the historical realization of the truth of human dignity, this journey will: (1) begin with the natural approach of Cicero; (2) expand with the Christ-centered thought of Saint Thomas Aquinas, revealing the immeasurable enhancement of human dignity from the Incarnation when God became man; (3) consider the influence of Immanuel Kant on modern thought by relating human dignity to reason, and; (4) examine the influences on the idea of human dignity as it came to be used in the Universal Declaration of Human Rights of 1948. We will give some thought to Mary Wollstonecraft, whose writings have become fashionable again under the influence of the feminist movement.

The Church has always firmly defended the dignity of humans through her teachings. We will review the teachings of some of the Church Fathers and saints in this regard. Then we will reflect on human dignity in Africa, a very important piece of world history, putting into consideration sectors such as life, tribalism, and racism.

In concluding this book, we will poke into an ideal society where human dignity is respected and valued for every individual. This will lead to an examination of what might be done to repair the abused condition of victims whose dignity has been trampled on by today's evil, thus denying them a full realization of being made in the image and likeness of God.

Chapter Two

The Image of God

Man and his existence in the universe have posed great controversies among thinkers and writers through the ages; a controversy which led Joseph Gevaert (b. 1930) to ask these questions: 1) What is man; 2) Who am I, and; 3) What is the sense or meaning of human existence?[1] These questions are the fundamental focus of philosophical anthropology and are present in all epochs at various levels of civilization. Today, they impose themselves with new urgency upon the consciousness of anyone who intends to live his human experience to the fullest.

According to the Yahwist view of who man is, in the book of Genesis, man was seen as Adam, fashioned by God out of "dust from the soil" (Gn 2:7). Also, it was recorded that God said, "let us make man in our own image and likeness" (Gn 1:26).

---

[1] Joseph Gevaert, "il problema dell'uanio; introduzione all'antropologia Filosofica," (Leuman (Torino): Elle Di Ci, 1992), 7.

Aristotle classified man as an animal in the class of *living things*. However, he emphasized that man's rationality differentiates him from all other animals. French philosopher, René Descartes (1596-1650), leaning more on self-consciousness, defined man as a *thinking thing*. Meanwhile, the Psalmist, after observing the wonderful nature of man and what he is made of, cried out in praise of man as "crowned with glory and splendor, little less than a god" (Ps 8:5; cf. Heb 2:6-7). Martin Heidegger (1889-1976) went on to assert that "man is the shepherd of Beings,"[2] which is in tune with Genesis Chapter 1, where man is given dominion over other creatures.

Contrary to Christian beliefs, Jean-Paul Sartre (1905-1980), an Existentialist, Phenomenologist, and Marxist philosopher, declared man to be "superfluous for all times;" "absurd;" "entirely gratuitous," and; just one among those "superfluous existences."[3] In other words, he does not see man as special.

Of all the above assertions by great thinkers and authors, the recurring theme centers on man and his dig-

---

[2] Sonia Sikka, Heidegger, Morality and Politics: Questioning the Shepherd of Being, (Cambridge University Press, 2018), 244.

[3] Gibbs, James. Reading and Being; Finding Meaning in Jean-Paul Satrtre's La Nausée. Sartre Studies *International* 17, no.1 (2011): 61-74. Accessed March 21, 2020 at www.jstor.org/stable/23512864

Chapter 2: The Image of God

nity. Having encountered diverse thoughts on *what is man*, this chapter will focus on two questions: 1) Is man really an image of God? 2) From whence comes the dignity of man?

Man, *ab initio* (from the beginning), is a being created by God. In the first chapter of Genesis, the creation account lays out the phases of creation as involving qualitative differences. It commences from the creation of light and darkness, then to the birds of the air, plants, aquatic and non-aquatic animals, and beings at large. Finally, there was the creation of a being based on a unique action of the Triune God. This action followed a divine statement, "come let us make man in our own image and likeness." (Gn 1:26) This statement conveys man as greater than other created things, for he carries the image and likeness of the Divine, hence an intrinsic dignity and rationality. In *The Catechism of the Catholic Church*, "the human person, created in the image of God, is a being at once corporeal and spiritual. The bible expresses this symbolically 'then the Lord God formed man of dust from the ground and breathed into his nostrils the breath of life, and man became a living being.' Man in his entirety is therefore willed by God."[4]

The International Theological Commission defined the image and likeness of God as "residing in the whole of man:

---

[4] *Catechism of the Catholic Church*, (Vatican City: Libreria Editrice Vaticana, 1994), §362.

his body and soul.⁵ This image of God doesn't make us God; rather, we share in the nature of Him Who created us. Therefore, to say that people are made in the image of God is to say that a gigantic qualitative gulf exists between people and God, where man is made up of a rational soul and physical body. Created in a special way by the Triune God, man has an inherent quality that made him able to dominate other creatures and be held at high esteem amidst other animals a quality we call *human dignity*.

The English word, *dignity*, according to Mette Lebech, comes from the Latin noun *decus*, meaning ornament, distinction, honor, glory. *Decet*, the verbal form, is related to the Greek δοκειν–to seem or to show, while the Latin participle form, *decens, –tis*, survived English language in the adjective, *decent*. In general, dignity is the standing of one entitled to respect. In other words, a being (in particular a personal being) induces or ought to induce such respect–its excellence or incomparability of value.⁶

---

⁵ International Theological Commission, "Communion and Stewardship: Human Persons Created in the Image of God," www.vatican.va/roman_curia/congregations/cfaith/cti_documents/rc_con_cfaith_doc_20040723_communion-stewardship_en.html.

⁶ Mette Lebech, "What is Human Dignity?" (A term paper by Mette Lebech, Faculty of Philosophy, National University of Ireland),

Dignity implies that each person is worthy of honor and respect for who they are, *not* just for what they can do. According to (*CCC* 357), "Being in the image of God, the human individual possesses the dignity of a person who is not just something, but someone."[7]

The state of being human entitles man to respect, a status which is intrinsic and must be taken as a given. In other words, human dignity cannot be earned, and it cannot be taken away. It is an inalienable result of the quality of our creation by God.

Affirming this, Saint Pope John Paul II (1920-2005), in his Apostolic Letter on the dignity and vocation of women entitled *Mulieris Dignitatem*, opined that "human dignity is inherent in the creation of humanity."[8] The difference between man and other animals lies in being created in God's image and likeness.

Human dignity should be the yardstick for assessing every problem relating to interactions of man in our contemporary world. David McCabe affirms this when he writes,

---

https://pdfs.semanticscholar.org/2a08/8148f2355c828597e6cfb96d10b635d9abe6.pdf, 7.

[7] CCC, §357.

[8] Pope Saint John Paul II, Mulieris *Dignitatem*, (Vatican City: Liberia Editrice Vaticana, 1988), §6.

"Most discussions of important moral and political issues, along with our every day reflections on how others should be treated, occur against a background assumption of human dignity–for example, the idea that human beings have special standing shared by no other creatures on earth. In countless contexts, talking about what we must provide to all persons (health care), what we must never do to anyone (torture), how to handle end-of-life scenarios (assisted suicide), what persons should be free to do (gay marriage), and so on, we can't get very far without running up against some claim about the dignity that each person possesses. Clarity on what that notion involves and the foundation of such claims, is thus a hugely important task."[9]

According to the *Catechism of the Catholic Church*, "Humans contribute to their own interior growth; they make their whole sentient and spiritual lives into means of this growth."[10]

Rational humans must be seen as possessing an existence that is incomparable to any non-human creature. Saint Pope John Paul II, in his first encyclical *Redemptor*

---

[9] David McCabe, "A Special Species," *Commonweal*, https://www.commonwealmagazine.org/special-species, June 17, 2011, 29.

[10] CCC, §1700.

Hominis, stated that "human nature, by the very fact that it was assumed not absorbed in Him (Christ), has been raised to a dignity beyond compare."[11] This inherent value must be respected by all humanity. This great value is clearly revealed throughout *Gaudium et Spes*, one of four Pastoral Constitutions of the Second Vatican Council promulgated by Saint Pope Paul VI. This document refers to "surpassing dignity of man, to search for a brotherhood which is universal and more deeply rooted."[12] In order for man's dignity to be recognized, there must exist an understanding that man is made to love and be loved. Love is the core of our creation in God's image and likeness. This ideal is unlike the current status quo in which man's inhumanity to his fellow man becomes normalcy. In his encyclical *Evangelium Vitae*, John Paul II wrote, "the sacredness of human life from its very beginning until its end . . . can affirm the right of every human being to have this primary good respected to the highest degree."[13]

Hence, man having understood his emergence and creation by the Infinite can be said to *represent* the Divine,

---

[11] Pope Saint John Paul II, *Redemptor Hominis*, (Vatican City: Liberia Editrice Vaticana, 1979), §8.

[12] Pope Saint John Paul II, *Gaudium et Spes*, (Vatican City: Liberia Editrice Vaticana, 1965), §91.

[13] Pope Saint John Paul II, *Evangelium Vitae*, (Vatican City: Liberia Editrice Vaticana, 1995), §2.

for he bears His image and was created in His own likeness. "I and the Father are One" (Jn 10:30 RSVCE).

Chapter Three

Aspects of Human Dignity

Violation of the right of another human being is an offense against the dignity of the human person and a denial of his due. According to Magid Khaddri, even in the Islamic religion, the five rights held by man are personal safety, respect for personal reputation, equality, brotherhood, and justice.[1] These rights emphasize the things one needs from others in order to maintain his dignity in the Islamic society.

The pressure in Western civilization to define the status of man grew out of awareness in Christian society of the dignity accorded him by the Creator and the recognition of abuses of that dignity. For peace to reign within the society, it became necessary to define the civil rights of man. Signi-

---

[1] Majid Khadduri, "Human Rights in Islam," *The Annals of the American Academy of Political and Social Science*, vol. 243: issue 1, 1946, 77-78, https://journals.sagepub.com/doi/abs/10.1177/000271624624300115.

ficant efforts by the American civil rights movement in the United States of America helped to advance this effort. Recalling the horrors of the French Revolution and oppression experienced at the hands of the King of England and his government, it is easy to see why the framer's minds were so greatly focused on resolving these matters. The result was firstly the Declaration of Independence beginning with the words, "We the people . . ." in 1776, followed by the Constitution of the United States of America in 1787. After its original passage, the Constitution underwent the addition of numerous other acts. Amendments thirteen, fourteen, and fifteen, which were passed in the years 1865, 1868, and 1870 respectively, are mainly related to civil rights. These Amendments came about as direct consequences of man's inhumanity to his fellow man.

This civil rights movement led to the eradication of slavery in the United States. Though it had been illegal in England since 1772, in 1807 it became illegal throughout the British Empire. This Abolition Law was further toughened in 1833. The 13th, 14th, and 15th Amendments to the U.S. Constitution introduced the principle of equality under the law and gave former slaves the right to vote. Slavery had robbed man of his freedom and right to flourish as human, treated these men as robots, and required them to give total obedience to the *master* while being unable to make use of his free will as a human person.

However, the eradication of slavery had side effects such as *segregation*, where people within a particular geographical area were kept separate based on color, race, age, education, and other factors.

In the United States of America, for instance, people of African origin, as well as Native Americans (Indians), due to their race and skin color were restricted from public schools, transportation, toilets, amongst other restrictions. This segregation created classes and differences in society which, up until today and despite the legal situation, have led some to be seen as inferior humans, not worthy of association. Even in public places, there remain those who see themselves as *Ubermensch* (Superman).

Segregation among humans is of two kinds: *de jure* segregation and *de facto* segregation. De jure segregation is mandated by law and enforced by the police to restrict access to places and facilities by those deemed inferior in the eyes of the ruling class. On the other hand, De facto segregation is a separation of the classes of people without any mandate by the law and without police enforcement. De jure segregation was fought in different places where it applied and was destroyed. This type of discrimination in action was when Rosa Parks (1913-2005) refused to give up her seat for a white man on a bus in Montgomery, Alabama, on December 1, 1955. This segregation led to a city-wide boycott of buses by African Americans, which caused the owners of the bus company on whose bus she rode to desegregate its buses. Very significant in rolling back segregation were the Northern students who came to the South by the busload, sometimes at the cost of their lives, to help protest against segregation.

We will examine in detail those factors which led to this deprivation of individual man's rightful dignity, undermining the equality of the human race.

The Differences Among Humans That Touch Upon Human Dignity

Race

Racism is the grouping of man according to particular physical characteristics which are resultant of the diverse society or environment in which they belong. This grouping creates a class so that a group of people is seen as second-class humans while the other sees itself as superior. *Grouping* based on inequality and discrimination all through history has considerably influenced how we relate to other human beings.

Race as a yardstick in determining whether or not a person is given his due is racial discrimination, that is, the unequal treatment of persons based on their race or ethnicity. In such situations, prejudice overrides justice, and a person is denied his right as a being with dignity. Racial discrimination has snatched from man, especially minorities, their freedom of association, employment, access to housing, credit markets, and consumer interactions.

Many Americans, for instance, continue to associate African Americans with laziness, being violence-prone, and welfare-dependence. Hispanics are often characterized as living in poverty, unintelligent, and unpatriotic.[2] Though these characteristics are evident in some of those communities, race is not necessarily the cause. Ben Carson (b. 1951), Secretary of Housing and Urban Development in the United States Government from 2017-2021–a former brain surgeon–amply shows the falsity of such assumptions. Another example is Senator Marco Rubio, who is of Hispanic descent.

Regarding employment, while some African Americans are still disadvantaged, others go on to triumph in their professions and commerce. Yet, there is a perceived disparity between the performance and achievements of African Americans and Anglo Americans. During employment interviews in individual businesses and despite Equal Opportunity laws, some employers use race as a factor to judge employee capacity. However, the idea of a degraded

---

[2] Lawrence Bobo, James R. Kluegel, and Ryan A. Smith, "Laissez-Faire Racism:The Crystallization of a 'Kindler, Gentler' Anti-Black Ideology," ed Stephen A. Tuch and Jack K. Martin, *Racial Attitudes In The 1990s: Continuity and Change*, (Westport: Praeger, 1997), 15-42.

civil status and racial inferiority of some African Americans is often taken for granted. This harsh reality sits oddly with the ideal espoused by Saint Pope Paul VI (1897-1978) in *Octogesima Adveniens*. He writes, ". . . . The members of mankind share the same basic rights and duties, as well as the same supernatural destiny. Within a country which belongs to each one, all should be equal before the law, find equal admittance to economic, cultural, civic and social life and benefit from a fair sharing of the nation's riches."[3]

Racism has proliferated in Africa over the past centuries due, in part, to boundaries created by European colonialism without regard for the people inhabiting those areas. As colonial powers departed, these African countries entered into both internal and external wars which resulted in racist attitudes and tribal warfare with the neighboring countries.

In Ivory Coast, there is a high rate of religious intolerance and inter-tribal hatred. Even Europeans visiting or residing in the area faced discriminatory actions and attitudes when, in 2004, the young patriots of Abidjan solicited for violence against foreigners and non-Ivoirians.

In Liberia, the country's constitution dictates that only those of Liberian nationality are to inhabit the area. This prohibition created walls for foreigners as only *bona fide*

---

[3] Pope Saint Paul V1, *Octogesima Adveniens*, (Vatican City: Liberia Editrice Vaticana, 1971), §16.

sons and daughters of the area were welcomed, creating an environment conducive to racial discrimination.

Likewise, Nigeria, known as the *giant of Africa*, has experienced its fair share of intertribal and religious wars, which led to the killing of millions in the Biafran War of the 1960s. Her population, which consists of both Christians and Muslims, has consequently encountered division based on religious values and practices. In turn, this led to discrimination, each side thinking along the line: *the others are not like us; they do not believe and practice our faith in the same way we do, so we must segregate them from us.* Likewise, the diversified nature of ethnic groups in the area posed a huge challenge as each one is different from the other. The formation of Nigeria by the British was, *ab initio*, an irrational assemblage of peoples without proper regard for their history, traditions, and abilities.

Racial discrimination flourished in African countries such as Namibia in the year 1904, when the Herero revolted against the German colonial rule and were later defeated by the Germans, thus leading to cruel suppression of the Herero. Tens of thousands were killed, directly or indirectly, through expulsion to harsh desert areas. Survivors were often enslaved, leading to the death of many more who lived in the camps.

In South Africa, during the years 1948-1994, the National Party (NP) Government enforced a system called *Apartheid* (Apartness). This form of segregation and racism limited the right of association, location, and movement among non-Europeans and other ethnic groups in the area. The oppressive system provoked massive opposition within South Africa (including from Europeans) and internationally. To further combat it and force the system to back down, many countries banned access to South African ships, aircraft, sporting teams, imports, and exports. South Africa became an international pariah.

Nevertheless, some neighboring African countries helped South Africa get around these bans and boycotts. There were strong arguments abroad that all the anti-Apartheid measures were doing was making the lives of the oppressed African people worse. Due to the resistance mounted by the African National Congress in conjunction with the weight of international pressure, the Government acknowledged that the *lid* could not be kept on the situation indefinitely. Accordingly, by a series of conciliatory measures, including the release of the A.N.C.'s former leader, late President Nelson Mandela (1918-2013), the system of Apartheid was dismantled and valid democratic elections took place. Mandela, now assuming the role of a grandfatherly figure, became the first President of the new Republic. He avoided much violence and bloodshed by insisting on authentic equality for all and also on a policy banning reprisals for past wrongs. It was a surprising and statesmanlike decision.

Chapter 3: Aspects of Human Dignity

The above listed countries are not the only countries that practiced racism, but to mention all and what they did is not our primary focus at the moment. It is pertinent to relate the above experience to the dignity of man; how it affects human dignity is the main factor leading to these segregationist thoughts and indifferent attitudes.

According to the U.S. Catholic Bishops in their work *Brothers and Sisters to Us*, racism is a sin that divides the human family, blots out the image of God from specific members of that family, and violates the fundamental human dignity of those called to be children of the same Father. Racism is a denial of the truth concerning the dignity of each human being as revealed by the mystery of the Incarnation. Racism is an arrow that pierces the dignity of man, for it degrades human dignity and mocks the Cross of Christ. As the US Catholic Bishops warned, "Let all know that it is a terrible sin that mocks the Cross of Christ and ridicules the Incarnation. For the brother and sister of our Brother, Jesus Christ are brother and sister to us."[4]

Further to the above, Archbishop Harry Flynn of the Archdiocese of St Paul, Minnesota, in his Pastoral Letter on

---

[4] U. S. Catholic Bishops, pastoral Letter on Racism, *Brothers And Sisters To Us*, (Washington D.C: United States Conference of Catholic Bishops, 1979) http://www.usccb.org/issues-and-action/cultural-diversity/african-american/brothers-and-sisters-to-us.cfm.

racism entitled *In God's Image*, asserted that "Racism is a serious offense against God because it violates the innate dignity of the human person. Since we cannot claim to love God unless we love our neighbor, we can only be one with God if we reject racism and work aggressively to remove it from our personal lives, our church, and our society."[5]

Therefore, man ought to work on his mind to create a change which, in turn, will reflect in his attitude toward the other. Man requires freedom of association with other men; that is what defines his existence and superiority as a higher animal with dignity.

Skin Color

A common justification for separating a group of people or individuals is due to their natural skin color which may be black, white, yellow, red, or other as the case may be. No matter how much it is justified, the practice is simply *discrimination.*

Skin color is a mechanism employed by the so-called *majority* or those considered superior, to segregate themselves from minorities. Often, one's skin color is used to

---

[5] Archbishop Harry Flynn, Pastoral Letter of the Archdiocese of St. Paul & Minneapolis *In God's Image*, (St. Paul: The Catholic Spirit, 2003), https://www.archspm.org/in-gods-image-pastoral-letter-on-racism/.

assign an individual or group of people to a *select* (the word interpreted pejoratively) status in society. For instance, the following thought process may occur: *I am white, and you are black. Therefore, due to the fact of our difference in skin color, you ought not to associate with me. You must be segregated, despite our common interests and friendship.*

This kind of segregation seeps into the laws and policies of a criminal justice system, business, employment, housing, politics, healthcare, and a host of others. When it comes to politics, one may not be allowed to exercise his or her franchise because his or her skin color is different from others in that society, automatically disqualifying the person from being a bona fide citizen of the community. The fallacy of this practice can be seen in light of the teachings in *The Catechism of the Catholic Church* which states, ".... Every form of social or cultural discrimination in fundamental personal rights on the grounds of sex, race, color, social conditions, language, or religion must be curbed and eradicated as incompatible with God's design."[6]

Many times, specific words are designated to those considered as either minorities or majorities in societies. For instance, names like *Jamal* and *Lakisha* signaled African Americans, while *Brad* and *Emily* were associated with Anglo Americans. Also, the word *nigger,* with its pejorative intention, had been commonplace.

---

[6] CCC, §1935.

Conclusively, skin color as an instrument of segregation or discrimination degrades human dignity. Saint Pope Paul VI, in the Conciliar document *Gaudium et Spes*, says, "Any kind of social or cultural discrimination in basic personal rights on the grounds of sex, race, color, social conditions, language or religion, must be curbed and eradicated as incompatible with God's design."[7]

Sex

The distinction between men and women according to their complementary biological endowments, male and female, is called sex. It is different from gender, which is a characteristic of words.

Sex discrimination bears similarities to racial and skin color discrimination, though it is more restricted than the others which are general in their application. It has become a highly politicized subject since the advent of the feminist movement. Segregation based on sex assures the privilege of one sex to the detriment of the other in a given place. An example is men-only clubs and, on the other hand, women-only clubs. Historically, this type of segregation is sometimes motivated by a desire, on the part of society, to protect women due to their perceived physical frailty compared to men. This type of discrimination can be either

---

[7] Pope Paul VI, *Gaudium et Spes*, §29.

Chapter 3: Aspects of Human Dignity

de jure or *de facto*; that is, either backed by law and enforced by police or based solely on social custom.

As the issue became politicized, the feminist movement sought to enforce for both males and females to have equal legal rights. Curiously, this quest has not been pursued with intellectual rigor. As a result, there are *women's refuges* where, of course, a male may not enter. Furthermore, special legal protections are sought in all manner of areas to protect women on account of their physical characteristics.

Most countries use this type of segregation as a means to protect females from sexual harassment and abuse in bathrooms, locker rooms, showers, and similar spaces, based on perceived need for privacy.

Some countries, like Germany, Korea, and China, have parking spaces reserved for women. Also, in Canada, the USA, Italy, Japan, and the United Kingdom, there are parking spaces set aside for pregnant women, for reasons of safety, of course.

The treatment of the two sexes in public law and custom has become fraught with difficulty in many countries. Compounding the struggle are the Marxist ideologues which promote the concept of gender under whose banner fall many policies/laws promoting a wide range of social engineering concepts, including the obliteration of the words *husband* and *wife*, *boy* and *girl*, *man* and *woman*. They struggle to make their way into politics and government regulatory bodies from whence they seek to enforce their ideas on the populace. These gender engineering efforts have achieved some success in the U.K., parts of the U.S.A., parts of Australia, and in New Zealand.

Age

Historically, age discrimination took place in most societies to protect either the aged and frail or the young and vulnerable, while taking into account the immaturity and inexperience of persons in their teens. Though this can be classified as positive discrimination, discrimination can be positive, indifferent, or wrong.

Age discrimination (or *ageism*-a rarely used term) began in the 1800s. It became necessary when the industrialization of England led to the monstrous use of children in coal mines. At that time, children as young as six years old were used as motive power to drag wagons of coal from the coal face to the surface, and as chimney sweeps' assistants, climbing up chimneys to clear blockages and clean them–often while the chimney was still hot. The Factory Acts of 1802 and 1819 in England were introduced to regulate this activity, limiting the working hours of children to twelve hours per day while children between nine to eleven years of age were limited to eight hours per day. Needless to say, those under the age of nine were no longer permitted to work. So, here we see discrimination intended to protect the vulnerable. When pressure was exerted to make children available for education, a Royal Commission in 1831 recommended that children eleven to eighteen years of age were to be limited to twelve hours of work per day. An argument can be made that it was not virtuous motivation that eventually did away with child labor, but advances in mechanization.

The law also regulated issues concerning those in their late teenage years, but not yet adults. In most countries, the age at which one can be conscripted or enlisted for military service is set at eighteen years of age. This policy led to the argument that if one was old enough to die for one's country, one should have the right to vote in the country's elections. As a result, in many countries the voting age was lowered from twenty-one to eighteen years. In the matter of driving licenses, a complex story unfolds. In most countries, people in their late teens, say from sixteen to eighteen years of age, are considered old enough to drive a typical motor vehicle. However, the high incidence of motor accidents among that group led some people to advocate raising the age to twenty-one years. So far, this does not seem to have been generally accepted–perhaps because of the potential loss of *votes* by the young during election.

Another area in which the young are affected by discrimination is the age of consent to engage in sexual intercourse. The age of consent in this area of law is based on several factors: 1) the age of onset of puberty; 2) the capacity of the young to financially care for any child conceived, and; 3) the level of maturity present to enable responsible and prudent choices. The law seeks to protect the young from predatory abuse by older people. Likewise, the customs and religious beliefs of the society are also powerful influences in determining the consent age. In different societies, there exist wide variations in the age of puberty. These variations seem to indicate race as a factor. In some societies, the onset of puberty occurs at age thirteen to fourteen years of age, whereas in others, it is as late as perhaps eighteen years of age. In this delicate issue, we can see that a simplistic approach would be inadequate. Also, when we research the history of this matter in various societies, we observe that opinion has developed very markedly over the centuries. Whereas many societies 800 years ago saw the need only to regulate the age of marriage and were happy to have that be as low as twelve years of age for females, in the nineteenth and even twentieth centuries, these age limits for all aspects of sexual activity–not just marriage–were adjusted several times upward in most societies. Now, in most Western societies, the age of consent is set at sixteen. In China and South America, however, it remains at fourteen years of age. In Argentina, it is as low as thirteen years of age, while in India and much of Central Africa, eighteen is considered adequate. It is worth noting that in a large number of countries, there is a discrepancy in the law as it applies to one sex or the other. In some countries, the age of consent is lower for females than for males, while in others it is higher for females. An example of the former is Kuwait, where females must be fifteen years of age and males seventeen (both only within marriage). Papua New Guinea is an example of the latter, where females must be sixteen years of age and males fourteen years of age.

At the other end of the age scale, there exists discrimination on those at the upper end of the age scale. Generally, the laws on this type of discrimination are intended to be protective of those affected. For instance, many countries set a minimum age for the receipt of State Aged Pensions. These laws were established during an era of industrialization when very harsh conditions existed during a long span of working life. At that time, society felt that the state ought to maintain those who had spent their entire working life supporting the state. Yet in this area, we find discrimination between males and females. In 2014, the thirty-four countries of the Organisation for Economic Co-operation and Development had an average retirement age for males at sixty-five years of age; for females, the average age was sixty-three and half years of age. However, changing demographics have induced steady increases in the retirement age in several Western countries. The percentage of older citizens has increased, and the effect of improved health care exaggerates the demographic trend, thus increasing the burden of the retirement benefits on national budgets. So, in these cases, we see the state diminishing the protection it affords the aged.

We cannot reasonably say that these are moral issues or issues affecting human dignity as long as acceptable levels of support are maintained. Such support seems to be the case in most countries today, with exception in countries like Nigeria, where although pensions are mandated and due, they are frequently not paid, paid irregularly, or after years of delay.

On the issue of older people, concerns which maintain that no one should in any way be affected in employment on account of his age, whether older or younger, should be put into consideration. Since 2000 in the European Union, it has been illegal to discriminate against a person on account of age in matters of employment, promotion, transfer, or in any other way. In 2004, Australia passed a much watered-down form of such legislation which contained many organizational exemptions and attached no criminality to violations of its statutes. It is hard to say how much real effect these laws are having, except in government employment. Anecdotal evidence may provide clues as to the effectiveness of said law.

In an Australian airline once belonging to the government and retaining a civil service mentality, the cabin staff is noticeably older than those in competitor airlines. When the matter is analyzed objectively, it can be deduced that an employer will, in many cases, prefer an older employee on account of their knowledge and experience. Conversely, a younger employee will offer the benefit of longer employment life and the possibility of being developed in the longer term for the benefit of the company. An additional benefit is, perhaps, greater flexibility in adapting to new ways. While these discriminatory concepts excite activists, most employees seem to be on the look-out for ways to retire earlier rather than seek protection to work longer years.

Education

Education is a tool of enlightenment which many are denied as a consequence of discrimination. It is inhumane when, through the restriction of his freedom of association and freedom to acquire real knowledge, a man is compelled to live without being educated about important things happening around him. Even in politics where man ought to exercise his franchise as a member of the society, he is prevented from participating, thus leaving him uneducated about the realities of the society in which he lives.

This hazardous discrimination limits one from an awareness of things around him and paves the way for government to create and perpetuate an educationally inferior minority.

Segregation of this sort prompted the assertion of Saint Pope John XXIII. In his encyclical entitled *Pacem in Terris*, he writes, "The natural law also gives man the right to share in the benefits of culture, and therefore the right to basic education and to technical and professional training in keeping with the stage of educational development in the country to which he belongs."[8] This view on education was reinforced during the Second Vatican Council. In the Pastoral Constitution of the Church *Gaudium et Spes*, it was emphasized that civic and political education is today necessary, especially for young people. As such, education should be provided to enable all citizens to make their contribution to the political community.[9]

Concomitants of Human Dignity

Right to Life

Chapter One of this book emphasizes that every man was created to live and is embedded with the right to live. It is thus a grave sin to terminate an innocent human life.

Right to life has become a hotly contested subject among medical practitioners, philosophers, ethicists, and other learned beings. It sprouted from issues like capital punishment, war, abortion, euthanasia, justifiable homi-

---

[8] Pope Saint John XXIII, *Pacem in* Terris (Vatican City: Liberia Editrice Vaticana, 1963), §13.

[9] Paul VI, *Gaudium et* Spes, §75.

cide, and public health care. Christian societies consider it taboo when an innocent person or group of people are denied their right to life through any of the above mentioned with the exception of war, justifiable homicide, and capital punishment. In these exceptional cases, the victim's guilt is assumed.

Everyone has the right to life, a gift from God. It ought to be protected by any law made in society for man. Where life is not protected by law, there is no room to enjoy other rights, and such society will evolve into an arena of struggle and destruction where one becomes wolf to the other. As rightly put by Saint Pope John-Paul II in *Centesimus Annus*, a society that denies this right cannot be justified, nor can it attain social peace.[10] According to Saint Pope John XXIII (1881-1963) in *Pacem in Terris*, any human society, if it is to be well ordered and productive, must lay down as a foundation to this principle, the conviction that every human being is a person, that is, human nature is endowed with intelligence and free will. Indeed, it is precisely because one is a person that one has rights and obligations flowing directly and simultaneously from one's very nature. These rights and obligations are universal and inviolable, so they cannot in any way be surrendered.[11]

---

[10] Pope St John-Paul II, *Centesimus Annus*, (Vatican City: Liberia Editrice Vaticana, 1991), §43.

[11] John XXIII, *Pacem in Terris*, §9.

To protect every individual's right to life is a must for society. As opined in *Caritas in Veritate* by Pope Benedict XVI, many people today would claim they owe nothing to anyone–except to themselves. Concerned only with their rights, they often have great difficulty in taking responsibility for their own and others' integral development. Hence, it is important to call for a renewed reflection on how rights presuppose duties if they are not to become mere license.[12]

Life is costly and precious. Therefore, any attempt made in the denial of this precious gift of the Divine tramples on the dignity of man and violates the laws of nature. Like the saying goes, *live and let live,* becomes a daily watchword.

Liberty and Pursuit of Happiness

From creation, every man was created equal with the same goal oriented toward the pursuit of happiness, both temporal and eternal. Any denial of this right to happiness may be likened to murder of the human spirit.

In 1776, when the beautiful words "life, liberty, and the pursuit of happiness" were written in the Declaration of Independence of the United States, the crowd erupted with joy because these words expressed what all people of good-

---

[12] Pope Benedict XVI, Caritas *in Veritate*, (Vatican City: Liberia Editrice Vaticana, 2009), §43.

will recognized intuitively. Those seven words call to mind God's gifts to man–of His desire for our eternal happiness.

A man's freedom and liberty must not be withheld or impeded by others, especially others in a position of authority. Rather, the government should serve as agents in maintaining these rights given man by the Creator. The Creator endows; the state protects. These rights can be forcibly suppressed or denied but can never be annulled or extinguished.

In exercising his liberty and pursuit of happiness, man should recognize his moral limitations by not trampling on the morally justifiable right of others in their own pursuits of happiness. One's freedom to pursue life, liberty, and happiness ends when it unjustifiably denies the right of others to pursue those same goals. Thus, the peculiar power with which a man can attain his goal lies in the application of reason.

Chapter Four

Abuses of Human Dignity and the Human Person

From the creation of Adam, man has been the masterwork of all things created–an extraordinary being whose worth made him master of creation. Any violation of that unique character that made man superior reduces him unjustifiably to the level of ordinary animals. An abuse of his human dignity is an affront to the essential personhood of man.

To stop man from enjoying his human rights absolutely, one must kill him. To a lesser extent, every assault on his human rights is a fundamental assault on his life. Human life is a precious gift from God and inviolable. Nobody has the right to take his own life or that of another; life is given by God and belongs to Him. On the value and inviolable nature of human life, Saint Pope John Paul II, in his encyclical *Evangelium Vitae*, opined, "The sacredness of life gives rise to its inviolability, written from the beginning in man's heart in his conscience . . . . man is always reminded of the inviolability of life–his own life and that of others–as something which does not belong to him because it is the property and gift of God the Creator and Father."[1]

Lately, humans are faced with a variety of abuses of themselves and of their dignity. Certain abuses confine man in a place and restrict his freedom of movement in order to gain a selfish satisfaction which may be monetary in the case of kidnapping. This type of abuse creates room for torture and maltreatment of the confined or abducted.

Due to dead consciences in the world today, man's dignity is abused and his life taken in the name of human sacrifice. Man, in this case, is slaughtered as a sacrifice to *gods* or *deities* based on the religion of certain societies in order to appease them. In other cases, this might be due to the desire for money and the level of insatiability in them. Some of these violations, and how they affect human life, liberty, and freedom, will be examined below.

Threats to life

Abortion

The *born*, wishing to be unencumbered in the enjoyment of their sexual pleasure, take the lives of those they

---

[1] Pope Saint John Paul II, *Evangelium Vitae*, (Vatican City: Liberia Editrice Vaticana, 1995), §40.

brought into this world as a direct result of their lustful behavior. Abortion is, without doubt, the most monstrous mass crime in the long and sorry history of mankind. Here at its essential level, we have the taking of human life for simple convenience. Abortion has made the very act of conception a contentious issue among ethicists. For, in seeking to justify this extermination of human life, they quibble about the commencement of life, generating a serious disagreement concerning the exact moment of conception. Equally, others have sought to raise issues concerning when the soul is implanted, and still others have taken a stand on when they deem self-awareness comes to the human person. These matters are hotly advanced by the enthusiasts for abortion, philosophers, religionists, ethicists, professional health practitioners, and hosts of others.

A great change, a conception, occurs at the very moment when the semen fertilizes the ovum during copulation. This change is the emergence of the human person, not a *potential* human person, but a *real* human being. Any intervention, then, with the intention of killing the child in the womb–an abortion–is the taking of human life. A fetus is only the name given to the baby at an early stage of its development in the womb. Naming this stage or any other stage, earlier or later, does not change the reality that we are dealing with a child who has been conceived and has the right to life that should not be violated.

In the United States today, a significant portion of its population believes that most abortions are a serious moral wrong, perhaps even murder. There is another significant portion who believe that many abortions are not wrong at all, or not so grievously wrong. Some people try to argue that a fetus is nonhuman because it has not attained consciousness or self-awareness. Therefore, they believe abortion is good and should be permissible. Consciousness and self-awareness are, in large part, matters of science. In this regard, both the scientific equipment used, as well as the techniques employed to study the child in the womb, are rapidly advancing. The Church does not consider consciousness and self-awareness as valid criteria for determining humanness or personhood. Nevertheless, consciousness and self-awareness of the intra-uterine child can be scientifically shown to be evident earlier within the womb. Philosophic and religious considerations have not, as yet, reached an absolute agreement. However, the moral teaching of the Church founded by Christ assures us, from the earliest days, that abortion is the murder of a human being.

Abortion deprives the victim of his or her natural development. Life itself is a gift from God and should not be violated or taken from an innocent human person–no matter the circumstances. As was rightly put by Saint Pope John Paul II in *Evangelium Vitae*, "life, especially human

Chapter 4: Abuses of Human Dignity and the Human Person

life, belongs to God; whoever attacks human life attacks God's very self."[2]

Some governments, in enumerating the rights of women, have designated the human fetus as non-human. They do so while seeking to end debates relating to the life of the human fetus. Some people assert that rights can only be awarded to those who have been born. For instance, recently in Ireland, once known as the *land of saints and scholars*, a referendum was approved that legalized the killing of fetuses in the womb. This news met with resounding cries of joy from many of her citizens upon hearing that abortion was approved in the area. Women laughed and hugged each other for the right to kill a child–a human person. That this is grotesque and contrary to nature needs not be said.

The human fetus is as much a human being at day one as it will be 9 months, 12 months, or 90 years after its birth. It is the same human being that is gradually and continually developing. God gave it life; no one has the right to interfere with that sacred life.

Rights to life are not judged on the basis of consciousness. Consciousness and sentience are complex, not black and white. Our judgments of beings as conscious or sentient are sometimes imperfect. The appropriate phrases should be "a greater or lesser consciousness and sentience."

---

[2] John Paul II, *Evangelium Vitae*, §9.

It is more reasonable to say a competent, healthy human person, or adult is more conscious and more sentient than attributing *nothingness* to fetuses.

Abortion is immoral and *contra-natura* (against nature), centering its intention on the termination and destruction of innocent human life. Some people may say that it is done to save the life of the mother when in mortal danger, but does anyone possess the right to judge which life is of greater importance? A bereaved mother refers to the fetus as *my baby* in cases of miscarriage, showing that the *thing* being called *non-human* is, in fact, truly human . . . be it from fertilization or even in the 7th month of pregnancy.

Genocide

Genocide[3] is a term coined by Raphael Lemkin (1900-1959), a Polish lawyer, in his book entitled *Axis Rule in Occupied Europe.* Derived from both a Greek prefix and Latin suffix, *Genos* is a Greek word that means *race or tribe* while *Cidium* is a Latin suffix which means *killing.* Merging both terms gives us the word *genocide*, which refers to the

---

[3] Raphael Lemkin, *Axis Rule in Occupied* Europe: *Laws of Occupation: Analysis of Government, Proposals for Redress*, (Clark: Lawbook Exchange, originally published in 1944, second edition in 2014).

killing of a race or a tribe. Also, genocide is defined as an indifferent and massive killing of a particular race or tribe which may be national, ethnic, social, or religious in nature. Genocide is perhaps the ultimate discrimination–going far beyond the traditional discrimination and segregation employed against such groups by race, sex, age, education, etc. Genocide does not have the goal of separating people into classes; its goal is the total elimination of the targeted classes.

Genocide is most times implemented by those with political power. They use their power in the state to inflict suffering on the target group, ethnicity, or tribe–especially on people of other geographical areas. These inhuman attitudes and all their consequential effects have set many tribes and countries at enmity with each other. Some have broken treaties, producing a lasting hatred on the part of surviving victims, thus paving the way towards continuing violations of human dignity and good order.

Blessed Pope Pius IX (1792-1878) in *Quadragesimo Anno* taught, "indeed all the institutions for the establishment of peace and the promotion of mutual help among men, however perfect these may seem, have the principal foundation of their stability in the mutual bond of minds and hearts whereby the members are united with one another. If this bond is lacking, the best of regulations come to naught, as we have learned by frequent experience. And so, then only will true cooperation be possible for a single common good when the constituent parts of the society deeply feel themselves members of one great family and children of the same Heavenly Father."[4]

Men ought to develop a rapport with each other in order to promote a good life and dignity. Achieving the *good life* consists of conversations between local, national, and international societies as regards health care, law, environment, science, business, religion, and other subjects which, in turn, bring stability and happiness for all races. To achieve this goal, the Church laid more emphasis on peace and mutual trust in her Conciliar document *Gaudium et Spes*, where it is written, "Peace must be born of mutual trust between nations rather than imposed on them through fear of one another's weapons. Hence everyone must labor to put an end at last to the arms race and to make a true beginning of disarmament."[5]

Much blood has been shed in the execution of genocide, accompanied by no apparent qualms–no apparent recognition–of the sacredness of the lives taken, or the dignity of the persons murdered. This has turned parts of the world today into an arena of combat to eradicate humans. Bangladesh is an example, where there exist mass killings by the Pakistan Armed Forces and its collaborators. The intent of

---

[4] Pope Pius IX, *Quadragesimo Anno*, (Vatican City: Liberia Editrice Vaticana, 1931), §137.

[5] Paul VI, *Gaudium et* Spes, §82.

Chapter 4: Abuses of Human Dignity and the Human Person   51

these collaborations was to stop the people of Bangladesh from gaining independence, but paved way for the shedding of very much blood in the area. In 1971, however, Bangladesh succeeded in gaining her independence only after the reduction of a great number of her subjects.

The same can be said of Cambodia, which lost a good number of her citizens due to agrarian ideology. This ideology led to forced labor and execution of many of its citizens between 1975 and 1979. An opposition group emerged in the Central African Republic in 2013 which centered its attention and attacks on the government, promoted political violence, and victimized those tagged as Christians and Muslims. Many of those targeted were killed.

Over the past decades, the Democratic Republic of Congo experienced severe wars and conflicts. These conflicts led to the death of many due to violence, lawlessness, decline in infrastructure, lack of food and good water, and poor sanitation which led to a vulnerability to certain diseases, such as the Ebola virus.

Nigeria is known for her large population and exports to the world, hence the name, *The Giant of Africa*. Unfortunately, she has faced a lot in her history, especially the civil war in the year 1967-1970 between the government of Nigeria and the secessionist state of Biafra. This war caused very great harm to the people of both parties, damage that continues until today. It is believed that 3 million Biafrans died, mostly from enforced starvation–including many children when the Igbo people in the geographical South felt they could no longer coexist with the Northern-dominated Nigerian Federal Government. As a result, they strived to achieve their own freedom under Biafra. Though the fight ended in defeat for Biafrans, it has, in effect, continued until today. In Nigeria, an Islamic sect known as Boko Haram has emerged and taken a radical stance, notionally against Western influence. Boko Haram continues to attack those known as *Christians* in the area, resulting in brutal killings.

In 1994, Rwandans faced internal wars when Hutu government extremists embarked on a mission to eradicate Tutsi minority groups from Rwanda. The motivation for this was Tutsi opposition to the Hutu government. The killings were horrendously barbarous, and figures given range from one-half to one million citizens. The same thing occurred in Iraq when the self-proclaimed Islamic State, popularly known as *IS(IS)*, attacked northern Iraq. This conflict, which centered on the ethnic and disagreeing Mohammedan sects and religious minorities, led to the loss of many lives.

There are also other countries that recorded atrocities which can be classified as genocide. Countries such as Mali, South Sudan, Sudan, Syria, Zimbabwe, and a host of others are examples of these genocides. Of gigantic historic proportions are the genocide in the Soviet Union of the Kulaks and the Jewish Holocaust in Nazi Germany. Both obliterated millions of people–the former for political reasons, the latter because of their race.

Human dignity has been a neglected reality in these areas where that genocide was experienced. There has been a cry for the respect of lives and a request for human rights in these areas. Unfortunately, voices can only be heard if–and only if–we call for adequate reflection and examination of consciences. Again, according to Saint Pope John Paul II's thoughts, as expressed in his work *Solicitudo Rei Socialis*, "If development is the new name for peace, then war, and preparations for war, are the major enemy of the healthy development of peoples. If we take the common good of all humanity as our norm, instead of individual greed, peace would be possible.[6]

Humanity cannot, out of greed and jealousy, wipe out the entire race in search of something that is, in reality, nothingness. Man must oppose class struggle and genocide by listening to the advice of Saint Pope John Paul II, who wrote, "Condemning class struggle does not mean condemning every possible form of social conflict. Such conflicts inevitably arise, and Christians must often take a position in the struggle for social justice. What is condemned is total war, which has no respect for the dignity of

---

[6] Saint Pope John Paul II, *Solicitudo Rei Socialis*, (Vatican City: Liberia Editrice Vaticana, 1987), §10.

others and consequently of oneself. It excludes reasonable compromise, does not pursue the common good, but the good of a group, and sets out to destroy whatever stands in its way."[7]

Human Sacrifice

Certain cultures which existed and still exist share a similarity in different societies. Though they may have different *modus operandi* (mode of operation), they are essentially the same. A feature common to certain pagan cultures is the human sacrifice to *deities*. Many things have been done in the name of appeasing the *gods* in their society, or their personal *gods*. According to W. Robertson Smith (1846–1894), sacrifice originated in *totemism*. Sacrifice was a communal meal shared between the people and their god who was their totemic animal and their kinsman. In his short entry in the *Encyclopedia Britannica*, Smith provides an explication of his theories of sacrifice, including those of human sacrifice.[8] Smith postulates two types of sacrifice. The first, the honorific, referred to a gift either on a friendly basis of exchange or as part of the homage to a powerful deity. The second, the piacular or expia-

---

[7] Saint Pope John Paul II, *Centesimus* Annus, §14.

[8] William Robertson Smith, "*Sacrifice*," *Encyclopedia Britannica*, 9th edition (Boston: Encyclopedia Brittanica, 1886).

tory sacrifice, took on a mystical, sacramental flavor when a tribe's own totemic animal was offered as redemption for a misdeed. This is a rather truncated view of sacrificial practice as is seen in the case of the Jews of the Old Testament who sacrificed birds and animals in accordance with the Law for purificative purposes, thanksgiving, seeking favor, or praising God. The ancient Romans, in their own pagan religion, sacrificed to discern the will of the gods.

Human sacrifice was normal in many lands for centuries, from the Pacific Islands to the Americas, Asia, ancient Europe, and to Africa. Human sacrifice is the killing of humans for the ritual purpose of appeasing the gods of the land. For Edward Burnett Tylor (1832–1917), the origin of religion lay in the primitive tendency to *animate* the entire world with *soul-ghosts*.[9] To him, humans offered sacrifice to release soul-ghosts who have gone to the world beyond. By doing so, they could join their ancestors in a sacrifice that also functions as a gift to gain a particular end, pay homage to a deity, or to use as a form of renunciation.

---

[9] Edward Burnett Tylor, *Primitive Culture: Researches Into the Development of Mythology, Philosophy, Religion, Art, and Custom*, vol. 1, (London: John Murray Publishing, 1871); and *Religions in Primitive Culture*, vol. 2, (Gloucester, Peter Smith Publishing, 1970), 1–87. The section on sacrifice (461–496) describes this phenomenon in terms of Tylor's views on its traits, mechanisms, permutations, and survivals.

Human sacrifice is the ultimate offering, for man is killed like an animal and even thrown to lower animals to feast upon as food, as a means to obtain power, control, and other selfish desires of those offering the sacrifice. Henri Hubert and Marcel Mauss in their essay on Vedic and Hebrew sacrifice, considered a sacrifice to be a religious act which, through the consecration of an offering, transformed the condition of the person who accomplished that act by joining the divine and mortal through the sacrifice. Self-sacrifice by God in human form is the ultimate ideal abnegation, an offering of the Divine Life.[10]

Anything that exists must have a cause and a sufficient reason behind its existence–except for the infinite and the unmoved mover (God). God has no cause but rather, causes all things to be. Some countries that practiced religions which required human sacrifice will be considered.

In ancient Chinese history, the Shang Dynasty, which lasted more than 500 years, helped in spreading this abominable act. Known for splitting the victim's body in two halves as part of the ritual sacrifice, they alternatively

---

[10] Henri Hubert, Marcel Mauss, *Sacrifice: Its Nature and Function*, trans. by W.D. Hall (Chicago, University of Chicago Press, 1981) is a short study of the structure and function of Vedic and Hebrew sacrificial rituals and is a classic work that has had widespread influence.

Chapter 4: Abuses of Human Dignity and the Human Person 57

used other body parts such as the victim's severed head. There was also the pit sacrifice which called for splitting young men and burying them. Again, there were foundation sacrifices which had children and infants as their victims, and also interment sacrifices meant for young women. Amongst these sacrifices, those captured in war and criminals suffered the most. According to David N. Keightley, the Shang political ideology believed the dead and the living formed a bureaucracy together. The dead received *salaries* in the form of human sacrifices for their task as intercessors between the king and the high god, *Di*. Without this, earthly prosperity could not continue.[11]

Historical records show that the early Mesopotamians would bury those from royal families together with their soldiers, handmaids, and servants. This was an honor to the deceased and enabled these servants to continue paying homage and serve their master in the afterlife. This practice can be traced to the Pharaohs of ancient Egypt. In order to make it easy for the sacrifice to be carried out, the household of the royals were poisoned a day before the burial so as have a successful interment.

The idea of sacrificing children to the deities can be traced back to the Maya and Aztec of the ancient Mesoamericans. They believed that sacrificing healthy children

---

[11]David N. Keightley, *The Origins of* Chinese *Religion*, (Berkeley: University of California Press, 1983).

determined what one would get from the gods. To please them, one must sacrifice a healthy and sound child. This led to taking good care of children for the sole aim of sacrificing them to earn favors from the gods. Many African countries indulged in this form of sacrifice and made this act rampant in places like Nigeria, Tanzania, Namibia, Zimbabwe, Uganda, South Africa, and many others.

In Africa, it is believed that when humans are sacrificed, it brings good fortune and luck to the person offering the sacrifice. In some of these African countries, when kings or men of prestige die, they are accompanied to mother earth with seven human heads or more, depending on the society. Some youths are sent (either inside or outside of their village) to hunt for heads so as to give the deceased a befitting burial.

Selling-off, for use in human sacrifice, of people with Albinism (congenital absence of any pigmentation or coloration in a person) has grown wild in places like Malawi and Tanzania. Sacrificing those with this biological anomaly is considered to bring luck as described by witch doctors in the area.

Human sacrifice, despite its evil and atrocious nature, is regarded as a tradition of some societies. On this ground, agencies such as human rights defenders and the African Charter on Human and Peoples' Rights called on the African Governments and the international community to ensure that potential victims are fully protected in their terrible vulnerability.

Human sacrifice is an offense to the dignity of man, reducing him to the level of an expendable animal. Man's rationality has organized the society to abuse it by inventing mythologies behind the worship of pagan gods. The *religion* lacks any authenticity or even rationality, and the efficacy of the sacrifice is out of the question.

Societies still enmeshed in this practice should quit viewing human sacrifice as a means to release souls for the service of dead ancestors. Stop seeing it as a gift that binds deities to people in an exchange that serves to propitiate gods. Stop seeing it as a communion meal through which life is assimilated and regenerated, as an expiation of past transgressions, giving human sacrifice a redemptive character. Stop treating it as a means of atonement, or as the means to attain earthly fertility or immortality. Stop seeing it as a means of transforming the human condition or unifying the divine and mortal. A stop should be put to dehumanizing ideologies which humiliate man and wage war against his dignity.

Indiscriminate Police and Military Attacks

The fight against discrimination and segregation remains incomplete if indiscriminate police and military attacks on civilians in every country, state, or society are not discussed. Of recent, it is acceptable in several countries to use security agencies to create problems in the very area they are meant to protect–making them the opposite of what they are called to be. Indiscriminate police and military attacks are intentional and unjustified attacks by the police or the military through the use of sophisticated or basic weapons. These acts can be carried out by means of aircraft, artillery, mortars, naval fire, missiles, or even the primitive baton to attack and harass innocent civilians.

A lot of societies today are no longer suitable for civilized habitation because of the misuse of power by those serving in security agencies. Still, the people often do not respond in kind when faced with such violence. However, *all* people and governments should respond vigorously, but constructively, to these forms of violence. The United States Conference of Catholic Bishops (USCCB) paper entitled *Confronting a Culture of Violence: A Catholic Framework for Action* states that we have "an obligation to respond. Violence . . . in our homes, our schools and streets, our nation and world is [sic] destroying the lives, dignity, and hopes of millions of our sisters and brothers."[12] This is

---

[12] United States Conference of Catholic Bishops, Pastoral Message of the U.S. Catholic Bishops *Confronting a Culture of Violence: A Catholic Framework for Action*, (Washington D.C: United States Conference of Catholic Bishops, 1994).

Chapter 4: Abuses of Human Dignity and the Human Person   61

easily said, but does not provide a ready response to retribution when the violence is perpetrated by the services of the State through verbal attacks, false arrest, intimidation, racial profiling, sexual abuse, and police corruption, all in the guise of being in control and having the freedom to intimidate. The USCCB noted that most often it is the weak and unfortunate, the poor, the aged, the young, minorities, and women who are forced to bear these injustices.[13] In non-Western countries, listing them is unnecessary because anyone is vulnerable to this arbitrary police/military action.

Discriminating against and brutalizing citizens has gone viral and is uncontrolled in many countries and has reduced some citizens to live in fear of those assigned to secure and bring peace and order in the land. The famous saying that "police are your friend" is now false in many countries, and people now try to settle disputes on their own due to fear of injustice and brutality. Most security agencies are used by those possessing power or by the rich in society to fight the poor, an injustice that leaves the gate wide open for exploitation. For instance, a rich man goes to high-ranking officers to pay some military personnel who

---

[13] United States Catholic Conference: Committee on Social Development and World Peace, *Community and Crime*, (Washington DC: United States Catholic Conference, 1978), 19.

will either protect or work for them. These officers are eventually used to threaten minority groups in societies.

Human dignity and liberty are at stake when justice and security are denied. The USCCB, in their work titled *Responsibility, Rehabilitation: A Catholic Perspective on Crime and Criminal Justice* states: "We must advocate on behalf of those most vulnerable to crime (the young and the elderly), ensure community safety, and attack the leading contributors to crime, which include the breakdown of family life, poverty, the proliferation of handguns, drug and alcohol addiction, and the persuasive culture of violence. We should also encourage programs of restorative justice that focus on community healing and personal accountability."[14]

It will be celebratory and a revolution when an end is brought to improper recruiting and training of those State Agencies which negatively affect the security of the people. Focus should be zoomed in on not only the voluntary aspect nor qualifications granted after physical training, but also on the social and intellectual aspects. This will ensure that instruction about human rights and a spirit of public service is inculcated. Also, there should be an active plat-

---

[14] United States Conference of Catholic Bishops (USCCB): Committee on Domestic Policy, *Responsibility, Rehabilitation: A Catholic Perspective on Crime and Criminal Justice*, (Washington D.C.: USCCB, 2000).

form that provides redress for unqualified and unfriendly agents, ranging from those in authority down to the rank and file. There is no society greater than that in which peace reigns, for *Ubi Caritas et Amor, Deus Ibi Est* (Where There is Charity and Love, There is God.). This motivated Saint Pope John Paul II to write in his message titled *The Jubilee in Prisons*, "We are still a long way from the time when our conscience can be certain of having done everything possible to prevent crime and to control it effectively so that it no longer does harm . . . perhaps humanity as a whole could take a great step forward in creating a more serene and peaceful society."[15]

Threats to Liberty

Slavery

It is believed that there is dignity in all work done by man and that it promotes the dignity of man, though this is not the case when work is instituted abnormally through forced labor, coercion, and mechanization of the human person. Among this sort of deleterious forced work, slavery is considered the most perverse abnormalities affecting his dignity.

---

[15] Pope Saint John Paul II, *Jubilee in Prisons*, (Vatican City: Liberia Editrice Vaticana, 2000), §5.

Slavery is an act that denies man his liberty and freedom by holding him against his will and compelling his forced labor through physical or mental torture. The enslaver establishes ownership of the other, thus reducing man to the status of mere property. In the past, laws permitted ownership of man as personal property. Some African societies endorsed this evil as a means of exchange with the North African Mohammedans. This practice lasted for some 900 years and even later with Europeans during the Triangular Trade. Humans suffered greatly at the hands of their fellow men during the Triangular Trade between Africa, America, and Europe with prominent roles played by people in different countries: the Dutch, French, Portuguese, British, Arabs, and African societies.

In ancient times, centuries prior to the birth of Christ, the enslavement of those conquered in war was the norm. Slavery was based strictly on conquest, through which the conquered were made slaves by the victors or sold to others as slaves. Later, as circumstances changed, specific factors came into play. The rise of Mohammedanism and its military conquests from around A.D. 600 brought about religion as a basis for enslavement. Those who did not submit to Islam were either killed or enslaved, particularly Christians. Due to high demand for slaves, there was massive capturing and selling of people into slavery. The Mohammedans crossed the Sahara by camel train to purchase West African slaves or sailed to East Africa to purchase slaves there. This went on for 900 years–a lucrative trade for those African Chiefs who had enslaved their brothers. People were sold into slavery when defeated in wars; some others became slaves as a result of unpaid debt. Borrowers were sold into slavery, and some were sold by their parents due to lack of finance, stubbornness, and too many children in the family.

Slavery strips man of dignity, liberty, choice, and free will, forcing him to work at the whim and purpose determined by his *master,* regardless of his own will. It was from this reality that Saint Pope John Paul II, in his work entitled *Centesimus Annus,* drew a modern parallel when he said: "Alienation is still a reality in western societies, because of consumerism that does not help one appreciate one's authentic personhood, and because of work which shows interest only in profit and none in the workers, considering them to be mere means."[16] It is true that formal slave trade is still in existence with over six million legal slaves in Mohammedan countries in Africa. Still, slavery eats deep into society today, even where it is long illegal. The psychological damage it wrought carries over for generations.

As earlier discussed, segregation came into being because of the existence of the slave trade, which in turn led to the assumption of inferiority of those enslaved and the

---

[16] John Paul II, *Centesimus* Annus, §41.

systematic oppression of this class for generations. Though the slave trade is now confined to only a few countries, primarily due to a lack of sellers and buyers of slaves, the world ignores what remains of the trade. Even countries that were former providers of slaves seem neither to care for nor sympathize with the six million or so poor wretches still enslaved. Organizations have sprung up to monitor these acts of inhumanity. Among those organizations performing this needed service are Amnesty International, Global Rights, and The Norwegian Refugee Council. Some religious groups in the church have taken the fight against slavery as their vocation. One such group is The Order of the Most Holy Trinity, in which its founder and members took, and still take, vows to liberate captives.

Without the necessary rights required for good standard of living, life is not being fully lived. The fight for the rights of man is the fight for his true life. Therefore, the struggle for the total abolition of this social evil is the proper responsibility of every man.

Human Trafficking

Over time, man has enslaved himself in a quest for higher standard of living. Human trafficking is the modern equivalent of formal enslavement. It is the recruitment, transportation, harboring, and reception of the human person through fraudulent and false promises. The ones

Chapter 4: Abuses of Human Dignity and the Human Person 67

perpetrating this fraud do so in order to exploit the person who is trapped. The tactics used involve generating fear through the threat of physical violence and even death.

As an illegal means for the exploitation of man, it often takes the form of prostitution of both the mature and minor, and forced labor which compels the victim to continually follow the wish of his or her master. The victim's redemption of his/her debts (usually via the *master's* charges for their transportation from their home country) is another aspect of this exploitation–an almost illusory hope of being free from the master, which takes years to achieve. In his letter to Archbishop Jean-Louis Tauran, Saint Pope John Paul II said; "Who can deny that the victims of this crime are often the poorest and most defenseless members of the human family, the 'least' of our brothers and sisters? In particular, the sexual exploitation of women and children is a particularly repugnant aspect of this trade and must be recognized as an intrinsic violation of human dignity and rights."[17] Human trafficking requires vigilance, as it can be ongoing in one's own immediate neighborhood, with no particular age group specifically

---

[17] Pope Saint John Paul II, Letter to Archbishop Jean-Louis Tauran on the Occasion of the International Conference "Twenty-First Century Slavery–The Human Rights Dimension to Trafficking in Human Beings," (Vatican City: Liberia Editrice Vaticana, 2002).

targeted. Both the literate and illiterate are vulnerable to modern enslavement as it thrives on desperation for economic improvement.

The deceitful nature of this sort of slavery is essential to its ability to attract people with empty promises of perhaps getting a nice job outside of their country. This is done through the aid of an organizer who lends the money for the passport and cost of the passage. Some people are promised good apartments and cars but end up forced into prostitution or into near-slave labor. In the case of more primitive victims, incantations may be performed before oracles to instill fear, accompanied by threats of violence, to prevent escape from camp or locations where they are assembled for transportation. Many victims are roped in through friends, brothers, and sisters. Others are actually kidnapped. The end result is that a victim is stripped of rights and turned into an indecisive being whose dignity is totally disregarded.

Irregular migration in the form of human trafficking and exploitation, particularly of women and children, must be condemned and prosecuted.[18] A thorough examination of the way people enter and leave a particular area, as recognized by both the USCCB and the US Federal

---

[18] Pope Benedict XVI, Message of His Holiness Pope Benedict XVI For The World Day Of Migrants And Refugees (2013), (Vatican City: Liberia Editrice Vaticana, 2012).

Chapter 4: Abuses of Human Dignity and the Human Person 69

Government, has sought cooperation with state and local governments in order to increase educational efforts so that all Americans will become more aware of this problem. Similarly, emphasis should be placed on the recovery and care of victims and on providing them with legal protection, social services, and repatriation as soon as possible. This is particularly true for child trafficking victims, who are most susceptible to the long-term horrors of this crime.[19]

Though movement of people across borders is part of a collective human experience, there exists an element of this experience that must be eradicated, i.e., the trafficking of human beings through the use of fraud, force, and coercion for the purpose of forced prostitution or forced labor.[20] To a large extent, the problem would be solved once the harsh conditions in the victims' home countries were resolved. On this issue, the Pope says, "I have always been distressed at the lot of those who are victims of various kinds of human trafficking, how I wish that all of us would hear God's cry: 'Where is your brother?' (Gn 4:9). Where is your brother or sister who is enslaved? Where are the brother and sister whom you are killing each day in clandestine warehouses, in rings of prostitution, in children used for

---

[19] U.S. Conference of Catholic Bishops, *On Human Trafficking*, (Washington, D.C.:USCCB, 2007).

[20] Ibid.

begging, in exploiting undocumented labor? Let us not look the other way. There is greater complicity than we think."[21]

Above all, everyone must be attentive, not only to the surface problem, but in addressing the real problem, which is dishonest, incompetent governments and their broken economies from which the victims seek escape.

Kidnapping

In the quest for riches and comfort, man does the unthinkable to satisfy his insatiable nature. To attain his desires, he pushes the boundaries of moral behavior, which may include kidnapping, which is a common crime in certain countries, states, and communities. This practice has existed for centuries. Kidnapping is the abduction, confinement, and/or maltreatment of a human person for the sole aim of receiving huge amounts of money, or some other type of *quid pro quo* (this for that), from those who value the victim. Confined by the victim's abductors, the victim may be subjected to different acts of maltreatment in order to incite fear, thus inducing the victim's co-operation with them in satisfying their demands. More commonly, abductors seek to extract a ransom from either the family or those with whom the victim has personal or business

---

[21] Pope Francis, Evangelii *Gaudium*, (Vatican City: Liberia Editrice Vaticana, 2013), §211.

connections in exchange for a promised release. Often, even when the ransom is paid, the victim is killed in order to conceal the identity of the abductors.

In some troubled countries, the government or a few heads of some organizations use this inhuman act to harm their opponents and rivals. They hire youths with a promise of huge sums of money if they kidnap opponents and confine them for ransom or murder. In some societies, this may also happen during elections, where an opponent is kidnapped in order to facilitate a victory for the organizer of the abduction.

Some countries experience kidnapping on a regular basis. Nigeria is an example of that. In fact, in Nigeria, kidnapping has become a regular business involving young men and women. Guns and other deadly weapons are used to entrap victims who are then sufficiently maltreated in order to meet their goals. After investigations obtain the financial strength of the potential victim's family, a ransom is requested from said family.

A considerable number of kidnap victims were abducted based on information given by people who know the victims. By objectifying the human person, this social evil harms man and his dignity. According to the Church document *Gaudium et Spes*, "Whatever insults human dignity, such as . . . slavery, prostitution, the selling of women and children; as well as disgraceful working conditions, where men are treated as mere tools for profit, rather than as free and responsible persons; all these things and others of their like are infamies indeed. They poison human society, but they do more harm to those who practice them than those who suffer from the injury."[22] Continuation of such acts denies human freedom and liberty for some people. Trying to stay safe forces one to live a life of exceptional privacy and not knowing whom to trust.

---

[22] Paul VI, Gaudium *et Spes*, §27.

Chapter Five

Respect for the Dignity of People

The creation of man, distinct and superior from all other creatures, warrants the extraordinary regard in which he must be held. Dignity, inherent in every human, requires respect from both the bearer and his fellow humans. That is why the Church, in promoting the proclamation of the Gospel message, her very *raison d'etre,* logically brings in its wake the defense of human dignity. "There is today no more urgent preparation for the performance of these tasks than: to lead people in the discovery of both their capacity to know the truth and yearning for the ultimate and definitive meaning of life."[1] In their mission for the protection and recognition of man's dignity, the framers of the Charter of the Fundamental Rights of the European Union, in the first article, required respect for and protection of the dignity of the human person. Here, the dignity of the human person is fundamental because it has value, it is respected, and, since it has a value, it must be protected.

---

[1] Pope Saint John Paul II, *Fides et Ratio,* (Vatican City: Liberia Editrice Vaticana, 1998), §102.

This dignity is not the honor we attribute to the high-class individuals in the community to show them how important they are to us. Rather, it is inherent in every human. According to Scripture, "When we deal with each other, we should do so with the sense of awe that arises in the presence of something holy and sacred. For that is what human beings are: we are created in the image of God" (Gn 1:27). This Scripture passage calls for the equality of all and recognition of the sacredness of each individual, which precludes any possibility of segregation. Respect is a result of the recognition of man's inherent worth. Each man has this intrinsic dignity that made him an individual person at the moment of conception. It does not depend on the other, though it requires the other's respect. As Saint Pope John-Paul II explained, human persons are willed by God and imprinted with His image. Their dignity does not come from the work they do, but from the persons they are.[2] The request for respect from the other is a call to recognize that *I am here,* and *I am human.* If you recognize only the worth in yourself and violate that of the other, it makes you unequal with him, thereby reducing him to sub-human status.

For human dignity to be understood and respected, we must be able to differentiate between intrinsic dignity and ethical dignity. Human dignity, inherent from conception

---

[2] John Paul II, *Centesimus* Annus, §11.

Chapter 5: Respect for the Dignity of People

and right from Adam, is inseparable from the human person, making man distinct from other creatures. Made *in the image and likeness of God* causes every man in society today to have his own dignity as human, regardless of sex, race, color, religion, or nationality. However, in ethical dignity, we discover it is man who accords this kind of dignity and the respect that flows from it based on how compliant his life is with the moral norms or principles of society. For instance, when one is a respecter of the norms of the society in which he lives, he is recognized as a prestigious being that deserves respect from others. He is accorded ethical dignity and respected in society. The respect accorded such individuals varies because the way one behaves and relates to the moral norms of the society may differ from person to person.

Attention must be paid to true dignity inherent in the human person rather than continue trampling on it and exalting the ethical dignity that is based only on the human facts of the society. As Pope Francis said in *Laudato Si,*

> "At times we see an obsession with denying any pre-eminence to the human person; more zeal is shown in protecting other species than in defending the dignity which all human beings share in equal measure. Certainly, we should be concerned lest other living beings be treated irresponsibly. But we should be particularly indignant at the enormous inequalities in

our midst, whereby we continue to tolerate some who considering themselves more worthy than others."[3]

Dignity is a state of worthiness, meriting respect on account of its divine origins. Since all men are equal, all men have dignity meriting 'respect.' Thus, respect should be the watchword and should be twofold in its application: respect for oneself and respect for the other.

When one exalts himself by acknowledging only his own dignity, without regarding that of others, he becomes morally vulnerable before God and before the society, as respect for the other is truly a concomitant of our human brotherhood. Mains indicated that apparent dignity exists when an individual is capable of exerting control over his or her behavior, surroundings, and society's treatment of them.[4] This means to checkmate one's behavior towards the other, as the now fading concept of *noblesse oblige* exerts its influence. On the respect for oneself and others, in reflection on ethical dignity, Haddock asserted that dignity is the ability to feel important and valuable in relation to others,

---

[3] Pope Francis, *Laudato Si,* (Vatican City: Liberia Editrice Vaticana, 2015), §90.

[4] Elaine D. Mains, "Concept Clarification in Professional Practice — Dignity," *Journal of Advanced Nursing*, 19: 947-953. doi:10.1111/j.1365-2648.1994.tb01173.x

communicate this to others, and be treated as such by others in contexts which are not perceived as threatening.[5]

To feel dignified is to be respected as a human with greater worth than the ordinary run of men. This situation is seen even in the animal kingdom; the deference accorded to the male leader of the pride of lions, to the bull elephant in his *family*. Here, the ascendancy comes purely from physical prowess and perhaps *seniority*. Man, as distinguished from the animals, shares different qualities, of which one is rationality. This makes him aware of the effects of the fundamental dignity given to him by the Creator. He must respect the other and, in return, be respected by the other in order to maintain a comfortable and serene society. This must be seen in all aspects of human life and activities, as indicated by Roberto Andorno in bioethics: "Since 1948 and the Universal Declaration of Human Rights at the United Nations, the notion of human dignity has operated as a central organizing principle of the international human rights system. It also plays a crucial role in the emerging global norms relating to bioethics, which present themselves as an extension of international human rights law into the field of biomedicine. The recourse to dignity in this specific area reflects a real concern

---

[5] Jane Haddock, 'Towards Further Clarification of the Concept Dignity," *Journal of Advanced Nursing*, 24: 924-931. doi:10.1111/j.1365-2648.1996.tb02927.x

about the need to promote respect for the intrinsic worth of human beings and the urgency to preserve the identity and integrity of the human species against potentially harmful biotechnological developments."[6]

---

[6] Roberto Andorno, "Human Dignity and Human Rights as a Common Ground for a Global Bioethics," *The Journal of Medicine and Philosophy*. 34. 223-40. 10.1093/jmp/jhp023, 2009, 56.

Chapter Six

Instrumentalization and Dehumanization of Man

Man is endowed at conception with an intrinsic value that is unique in each individual person. It calls for reciprocal respect from his human brothers, thus creating a civilized standard association serving all men in the society in which he lives. In previous discussions, we examined certain ways by which man can be excluded from this common association that exists in society, through racial discrimination, stereotyping, sex, age, and a host of other factors. We also looked at the creation of man, the emanation of this vital value in him, and the distinctive nature that separates him from mere animals. It is on this backdrop that it becomes necessary to examine how man, when his fundamental dignity is violated by his fellow humans, becomes an instrument, means, or an object through which an end can be actualized.

What is an *instrument* in this context? In the normal usage of an instrument, it is a tool, especially one for a precise task. After the use of these instruments to achieve the sole aim of the user, it is not put into consideration again until when next it is needed. Its only value lies in its limited utility.

The instrumentalization of a human being is the reduction of man by his fellow man to the level of such a tool or implement for the realization of an end. He is used to achieve a certain goal without consideration of his consent. We employed the word *used* because he is exploited and cast aside, disregarded, when the end has been achieved–his only value to his user is the self-centered motivation of achieving an end result. The Principle of Sufficient Cause tells us that everything that happens has a reason. Now, if one human treats another as if he has no value other than to serve his immediate purposes, he has degraded the other, reduced him to the status of a mere instrument. For then, his only reason for being, as far as the user is concerned, is to satisfy his immediate purpose.

It is also certain to say that the instrumentalization of the human being gives room for his dehumanization. When one is used without his consent, he is reduced to the level of an object to be used anytime. Saint Pope John Paul II has written:

> "The exercise of solidarity within each society is valid when its members recognize one another as persons. Those who are more influential, because they have a

greater share of goods and common services, should feel responsible for the weaker and be ready to share with them all they possess. Those who are weaker, for their part, in the same spirit of solidarity, should not adopt a purely passive attitude or one that is destructive of the social fabric but, while claiming their legitimate rights, should do what they can for the good of all. The intermediate groups, in their turn, should not selfishly insist on their particular interests, but respect the interests of others."[1]

Dehumanization is the stripping off of the humanity of man. This may be done through words or action to reduce him to the level of non-humans so that it is possible to truly use him as an object and deny his human dignity.

Words ought to have a very great consideration in the fight and pursuit of the dignity of the human being, as man is dehumanized through the use of some exclusive words to force him out of the community where he belongs. The way a sentence is constructed matters a lot; it can exclude a person from the society of beings with dignity as pointed out in *Populorum Progressio.*

"Each man is a member of society. He is part of the whole of mankind. It is not just certain individuals but

---

[1] John Paul II, Solicitudo Rei Socialis, §39.

all men who are called to this fullness of development. Civilizations are born, develop, and die. But followers of Christ must assist humanity in advancing along the path of history. Humans have inherited from past generations and benefitted from the work of some contemporaries: for this reason, we have obligations towards all and cannot refuse to interest ourselves in those who will come after us to enlarge the human family. The reality of human solidarity, which is a benefit for us, also imposes a duty."[2]

Actions too can degrade a person and be used to demean man amidst his fellow men. One's actions towards the other reveal a great deal about one's conception of the particular man in question.

There are essential rights that must be accorded humans to obstruct dehumanization efforts to objectify man. These rights include identity, respect, and freedom of association. In his identity, man is shown to be unique, independent, and has God-given free-will. Here, he is the master of his own existence and decides how to live his life in a manner he believes will be beneficial and not detrimental to him, and consistent with his obligations in the society. To respect someone means to give to another the

---

[2] Pope Paul VI, Populorum *Progressio*, (Vatican City: Liberia Editrice Vaticana, 1967), §17.

recognition of the dignity and innate value of each human being, which is degraded by the denial of such recognition. Here, man is calling the other to free him from everything which oppresses his rights. By freedom of association, we refer to the right to develop inter-dependency and unity that is meant to exist among men, making them flourish through the exchange of certain potentials to better the human society.

Dehumanization excludes man from a common association in a society which may come in the form of racism, genocide, age, and other factors mentioned in previous chapters. The Catholic Church, through the Second Vatican Council, stated that a sense of responsibility will not be achieved unless people are so circumstanced that they are aware of their dignity and are capable of responding to their calling in the service of God and of humanity. For true freedom is often crippled by extreme destitution, just as it can wither within ivory tower isolation brought on by overindulgence in the *good things* of life. It can, however, be strengthened by accepting the inevitable constraints of social life, by undertaking the manifold demands of human relationships, and by service to the community at large.[3]

One must pay tribute to nations whose systems permit the largest possible number of their citizens to partake in

---

[3] Paul VI, Gaudium *et Spes*, §31.

public life in a climate of genuine freedom.[4] The advice of Pope Emeritus Benedict XVI is worded thus,

> "Subsidiarity is first and foremost a form of assistance to the human person via the autonomy of intermediate bodies. Such assistance is offered when individuals or groups are unable to accomplish something on their own, and it is always designed to achieve their emancipation because it fosters freedom and participation through assumption of responsibility. Subsidiarity respects personal dignity by recognizing the person a subject who is always capable of giving something to others."[5]

In his discussion about man, society, and dignity of labor, Karl Marx fought earnestly in the use of man as an object or means to an end, which he believed was an inevitable feature of the capitalist societies of his day. From this jaundiced view, he developed his ideas of inevitable class warfare. He frowned upon the exploitation and alienation of humanity within society, which reduces the lower class (*proletariat*) to the level of the machines and robots that can be found in work places owned by upper-class citizens, known as the *bourgeoisie*. Ironically, Marx, who

---

[4] Ibid.

[5] Benedict XVI, *Caritas in Veritate*, §57.

never had a job in his life, inspired Socialism and Communism which, between them, perfected the dehumanization of the working class and thoroughly instrumentalized them for the purposes of creating a new order of economic reality but resulted in the enslavement and death of tens of millions in the former Soviet Union, in the National Socialist Germany, and in Communist China.

There is honor in the work that man does, but not when its circumstances exploit his dignity. It is necessary for the government to set up the means of regulating working conditions to prevent labor exploitation. As stated by Saint Pope John XXIII, and also demanded by the common good, civil authorities must make efforts to bring about a situation in which individual citizens can easily exercise their rights and fulfill their duties. For experience has taught that, unless the authorities take suitable action with regard to economic, political, and cultural matters, inequalities between the citizens tend to become more and more widespread. This is especially so in the modern technological world. As a result, human rights are rendered totally ineffective, and the fulfillment of duties is compromised.[6]

---

[6] John XXIII, *Pacem in Terris*, §63.

Chapter Seven

Practices that Violate Human Dignity

Man organized several habitations to realize the essence of his existence, to be happy, and also make the other happy in line with the mind of the creator. This creation of different habitations eventually gave rise to several languages, cultures, and races.

To realize the aim of creating these different societies, man enacted laws comprising rules and regulations guiding people in society. It also helped in eradicating from society the ill practices which pose as a place of combat between man and his fellow man, giving room to man's inhumanity to his fellow man.

Man has superiority over other beings which exist with him in society, be it living or non-living beings. His rationality also differentiates and classifies him as a higher animal to be held in high esteem by both the things under them and also by their creator. Instead, in the same society which man created as means of realizing who he is, i.e. a being with dignity, he is now exploited and excluded from the place he created for his happiness. Likewise, laws are enacted to stand against a particular set of people, especially those considered minorities by those who see themselves as the majority, or the superior ones in the society. Man is tortured, raped, and exploited through that labor which is supposed to be the definer of his dignity and is at last excluded from the society where he lives with his fellow man.

Most societies are no longer conducive for habitation due to adoption of abnormal practices. These practices have caused the migration of people and the violation of their dignities. In all, it is to be noted that these practices are enacted to extort and exploit the potentials and dignity of those considered as minorities and inferior humans and can only take place as a result of collective acceptance of the very act or through the utterance of those in authority.

Social Exclusion

God made man the shepherd and master of all creatures, both living and non-living things. After man's creation, God kept man in the universe to stay and care for one another which led to the emergence and expansion of human society.

The creation of society gave rise to interdependence among men due to a need for rapport with others as one family, according to the classification of things by Aristotle.

Chapter 7: Practices that Violate Human Dignity

For man to live in harmony with others there must be a common association.

Today, man's inhumanity to the other, which made him be seen as *homo homini lupus* (man-wolf to his fellow man), has eradicated the common association that existed among men, and turned society into an arena for battle and segregation. Instead of being a ground for multiplication of humans, society has become a place where humans are seen as an abomination, killed like ordinary animals. At the same time, racism, color, and other differential factors have become a welcoming reality in human society. Society is now a place for the survival of the fittest, where certain men see themselves as superior to the others, leading them to overshadow, instrumentalize, and dehumanize them. This gave rise to the emergence of the social exclusion existing in human society today. It warrants a look into what it is and how it has harmed society, man in particular.

The phrase *social exclusion* was introduced as an academic debate in the late twentieth century as a theoretical concept for the reflection on the situation of those not seen as humans and, thus, segregated. Social exclusion is a descriptive of preventing people from participating fully as members of human society. Rather, such people are seen as dispensable human mass. In this case, the minority group is seen as superior to the socially excluded persons in society. These men are only used to complete the population of an area, but when it comes to the rights that belong to human beings, they are totally excluded from it. For instance, in some societies, those born out of wedlock are not accepted as members of the particular society where they reside. They are seen as strangers inhabiting a geographical area.

According to Pope Paul VI, each man is a member of society. He is part of the whole of mankind. It is not just certain individuals, but all men who are called to this fullness of development. Civilizations are born, develop, and die, but humanity is advancing along the path of history like the waves of a rising tide, gradually encroaching on the shore. We have inherited from past generations, we have benefited from past generations, and we have benefited from the work of our contemporaries within those generations. For this reason, we have obligations towards all. We cannot refuse to take an interest in those who will come after us, to enlarge the human family. The reality of human solidarity, which is a benefit for us, also imposes a duty.[1] Exclusion causes some sort of mental illness which, according to researchers, may lead to the isolation of oneself of which suicide is the effect of such action. The exclusion of man from human society leads to the denial of his dignity as human. The love that should be intertwined in the associations of men within society is denied and removed at the exclusion of a human being.

---

[1] Pope Paul VI, *Populorum Progressio*, §17.

Culture or norms stand against the dignity of humans by encouraging a selective standard of human society. For him whose dignity is violated, his rights, the respect due to him, and the common association between him and his brothers are also denied him. Therefore, live and let others live. For all are one through the Creator.

Torture

Not considering the kind of treatment received by man through the violation of his dignity is more or less like recording a war without considering the kind of weaponry used. It renders the war story woefully incomplete. As regards the violation of man's dignity, inhuman treatment reduces him to the level of common animals. In the case of torture, what are the weapons used? What are the institutions, practices, and agencies of dehumanization that employ those weapons?

To begin with, what is torture? It is not easy to articulate a particular definition of this kind of practice, as it is comprised of a wide range of acts which are used to maltreat someone in an effort to extract the truth behind an action done, or for the sake of segregating one from a common group in society.

Torture is the infliction of physical and/or mental pain and misery. Through severe beatings and/or the use of special devices, the victim of the torturing is stressed, weakened, and *incentivized* to provide information that would not otherwise be forthcoming, for any number of reasons. Other potential goals for this type of practice are: 1) force the victim to carry out certain work which is against the victim's wishes; 2) *re-educate* someone so that they will behave or think in a manner desired by the torturers, or 3) convince the victim to perform a future act they are not currently willing to do. These are not the only possible reasons that someone might use torture as a weapon. Torture is common around some security agencies, such as the police or the military. Sometimes, the sole aim for the practice is the protection of both society and those living in it.

Here is another example of a common type of torture. During the course of a trial, a witness may be taken to another location, either within or outside of the court building, for the purpose being vigorously interrogated by those desiring to obtain the *truth* from him or her. The witness, or defendant, as the case may be, can end up staying for days. The interrogators may employ special devices, such as scissors, knives, needles, or devices used to generate electrical current on the defendant. These various devices may be used on the person's private parts, or other sensitive areas of the body, to convince the witness to provide the "proper" explanation for the circumstances surrounding actions taken.

Also, torture can be performed by certain groups set up by society to maintain peace and order, groups outside of the security agencies instituted by the state itself. This is in some African societies where, for instance, the youths are asked to maintain peace and serenity in the society. In these situations, people who are caught violating the laws of society, e.g., kidnapping, rape, stealing, are subjected to different kinds of maltreatment up to and including death. The goal here is not to discover the truth, but to keep the peace, so to speak. This type of treatment doesn't simply trample upon the dignity of the accused (who have not been proven guilty of a crime), but it destroys it. What is worse, this kind of maltreatment is sometimes used on suspects and, in some cases, on the innocent. When these brutal practices are employed, the tortured person is forced to admit to a crime, even though he or she had no involvement in said crime.

The torturing of any human being dehumanizes its victim, making it wicked. There are other ways of obtaining the truth from suspects that do not involve the destruction of their human dignity. There is a need for the utilization of trained professionals in these judicial sectors. Proper investigations must be conducted in order to obtain the tangible and physical facts necessary to determine the guilt or innocence of a suspect. Doing so will lessen the likelihood of inflicting pain and degradation on the innocent. Following the views of the USCCB on this matter, it is morally unsatisfactory and socially destructive for criminals to go unpunished, but the forms and limits of punishment must be determined by moral objectives which go beyond mere inflicting of pain and injury on the guilty. Thus, we would regard it as barbarous and inhumane for a criminal who tortured or maimed a victim to be tortured or maimed in turn. Such a punishment might satisfy certain vindictive desires of the victim, the family of the victim, or the public, but the satisfaction of such desires is not and cannot be an objective of a humane and Christian approach to punishment. The forms of punishment to be used must be determined with a view to the protection of society, its members, and to the reformation of the criminal and his reintegration into society (which may not be possible in certain cases).[2]

Therefore, maltreatment harms the dignity and right of man. Why? It is because maltreatment turns the will of the victim against the victimizer, who is exposed as prey to his hosts by not knowing what to do to rescue himself from such treatment or to prove his innocence as in the case of innocents.

---

[2] USCCB, *Statement on Capital* Punishment, (Washington, D.C.:USCCB, 1980), §1.

Rape

Rape, throughout history, is viewed in different epochs by professionals on moral issues. It is an assault that leads to the sexual maltreatment of man, which in turn stands against his dignity. This assault on human dignity is common towards women, both young and old. The damage produced deeply affects the sensitive part of their personality.

The word *rape* etymologically originated from the Latin word *rapere*, which means to grab or snatch. In the fourteenth century, it came to mean to seize or to take away forcefully. Expanding on that, it literarily means to take away forcefully the vital aspect of man which is hidden in his sexuality. It can also be seen as a type of exploitation that involves forceful sexual intercourse by a perpetrator or the use of some object to penetrate into a human body, more often than not, the body of a woman, which occurs without the consent of the victim.

In this violation of man's dignity, the lack of the victim's consent is the keyword, for it defines in totality what rape really is. Any sexual intercourse that exists outside of the consent of the other is rape. Free intercourse must involve an agreement between the two parties involved in the act. This agreement is the respect of the dignity of both, for anything outside this is rape and an act of using the other. This act of violence may come from a date, a relation, or any adult against the young.

This systematic means of violating the rights of a human can be seen in rape, incest, battery, prostitution, sexualized torture, and sexualized murder. Sexualized torture and murder points at the use of physical force to exploit the sexuality of the victim, whereby the perpetrator uses objects to frighten in order to penetrate him or her. In attempting to intimidate, if the victim proves stubborn despite the physical force applied, the violator might murder out of anger and annoyance of resistance.

Using someone as a means to actualize the achievement of certain goals, but doing so without the consent of the user, will lead to the violation of the dignity of the person used. Forceful sexual exploitation can lead to psychological trauma, sickness, and even unwanted pregnancy, as it is not the wish of the victim. Failure to regard rape as gender-based violence leads to the total violation of women's rights and dignity.

Absolute Poverty

Poverty is a negation of the actual need of man. When we talk about the practices that violate human dignity, we consider poverty as one of those practices, though it is not sometimes intentionally caused by the other of his fellow humans. This is not like the harm caused by the *act* of raping, rather it is an intentional or unintentional omission of that which is necessarily needed by the other to live an acceptable standard of life, as required in the community. Despite the omission of the necessary need of the other unintentionally, it is sometimes made intentional in order to put an individual or group of individuals who are considered undesirable into a minority class that requires "help" by society wherein the elected officials use the poor as a means of ensuring a power base upon which they win elections.

Intentionally produced poverty violates another's human dignity. It incentivizes people to remain in poverty–to not help themselves and to remain dependent on others for their survival in all its aspects. Once entrenched, governments can use this power base to enact other laws which can further depredate human dignity to atrocious degrees. An argument can be made that both abortion and artificial birth control came into widespread existence as a *direct result* of this practice.

In situations requiring the making of rational choices and decisions, poverty kills the will power of an individual, making him indecisive in nature. Before making any decision relative to survive, the impoverished must seek the advice and approval of those who help support. They have become dependent and, therefore, want to avoid any possibility of their abandonment. After all, who in their right mind would want to die of starvation or lose their shelter?

Here is a hypothetical example: Jack is rich. Jacob benefits exclusively from the aid of Jack to survive. If Jacob should decide to start schooling, he must get the funds from Jack to do so. However, if Jack believes that it is in his best interests to keep Jacob uneducated, Jack will come up with an excuse to say no. In this example, Jacob has given up his ability to control his own attempts to pursue success or experience failure. If one is allowed to exercise his will power, his dignity will never be violated, and there will be oneness in human society. As Pope Benedict XVI tells us, within the community of believers, there can never be room for a poverty that denies anyone what is needed for a dignified life.[3]

The human dignity owed to each person provides the room for man to decide how he or she chooses to live. When one's decision and plans are limited and regulated by the other, it enables exploitation and dehumanization of the human person, which leads to the violation of his dignity. According to the USCCB, working for the common good requires us to promote the flourishing of all human life and all of God's creation. In a special way, the common good requires solidarity with the poor, who are often without the

---

[3] Pope Benedict XVI, *Deus Caritas Est*, (Vatican City: Liberia Editrice Vaticana, 2005), §20.

resources needed to face the many problems they may encounter, including the potential impacts of climate change. Our obligations to the one human family stretch across space and time. They tie us to the poor in our midst and across the globe, as well as to future generations. The commandment to love our neighbor invites us to consider the poor and marginalized of other nations as true brothers and sisters. As such, they must be allowed to share with us the one table of life, which is intended by God for the enjoyment of all.[4]

Sometimes, the bourgeoisie (the *elite*) in society causes things to happen that are proximately or incidentally detrimental to the poor. The result may lead to the violation of human dignity as opined by Pope Francis in his popular encyclical, *Laudato Si.* In it he says, "In fact, the deterioration of the environment and of society affects the most vulnerable people on the planet: 'Both everyday experience and scientific research show that the gravest effects of all attacks on the environment are suffered by the poorest.' For example, the depletion of fishing reserves especially hurts small fishing communities without the means to replace those resources; water pollution particularly affects the poor who cannot buy bottled water, and rises in the sea

---

[4] USCCB, Global Climate Change: A Plea for Dialogue, Prudence, and the Common Good, (Washington, D.C.: USCCB, 2001), 25.

level mainly affect impoverished coastal populations who have nowhere else to go. The impact of present imbalances is also seen in the premature death of many of the poor, in conflicts sparked by the shortage of resources, and in any number of other problems which are insufficiently represented on global agendas."[5] This sometimes makes it impossible for the poor to freely exercise their right of freedom or to partake in the political sectors of society when the poor are not seen as belonging to the same class as the rich in society. This strategy encourages the rich to continue getting richer and the poor to continue getting poorer.

Building a society in which love is put into practice by caring for and accommodating the less privileged will lead to the elimination of any omission of any acts that are needed for all of its population to maintain their dignity as human persons created in the image and likeness of God. We would do well to heed the advice of Pope Francis (b. 1936) when he tells us that our current world, where injustices abound and growing numbers of people are deprived of basic human rights and considered expendable, requires our immediate acceptance of the principle of the common good of man. Said principle is, both logically and inevitably, a summons to solidarity and a preferential option for the poorest of our brothers and sisters. This

---

[5] Pope Francis, Laudato Si, §48.

option entails recognizing the implications of the universal destination of the world's goods. Pope Francis demands before all else an appreciation of the immense dignity of the poor in the light of our deepest convictions as believers (cf. *Evangelii Gaudium* §123). We need only look around us to see that, today, this option is, in fact, an ethical imperative essential for effectively attaining the common good.[6]

Labor Exploitation

Through the work of human hands, man's dignity can be seen. It is through the work of those same human hands that his dignity can be violated. Anything man does to another without his consent is exploitative in nature. As discussed in previous chapters about threats to liberty, such as slave trade, human trafficking, etc., hard labor is one of those threats used to violate the human dignity of man. Forced labor was used on prisoners of war and slaves bought from Africa. Pope John Paul II believed that a human society is both alienated and alienating if its organizations, means of production, and societal consumption make the transcendence of human dignity more difficult.[7]

---

[6] Ibid., §158.
[7] John Paul II, *Centesimus Annus*, §41.

Labor exploitation is the maltreatment of workers in ways that violate their human dignity for the sole purpose of using them for the achievement of mass production of goods in the workplace. Here, the sole aim of maximizing output is achieved by converting man into an instrument through which the realization of an end is accomplished. While this end can be achieved humanely, too often it is not.

Karl Marx, who solicited for the fair treatment of workers in factories and other types of workplaces, saw labor exploitation as a means of violating man, thereby converting him to nothing more than a robot or machine used by the company for mass production. Marx was not comfortable with the way the bourgeoisie mistreated the workers in their places of work. As an example of his view of exploitation, let's use a hypothetical bakery. In this bakery, arriving workers first remove their clothes and put on the one's used by the bakery. This was done in an environment where their dignity was embarrassingly compromised. To maximize production, their phones are taken away and their bathroom breaks are limited. A day's work (from 6:00am to 6:00pm) may produce about five-thousand loaves of bread, none of which go the employees (except for the burnt ones). Both incoming and outgoing employees are subject to search (an assumption of guilt is the implied message here). The factory was in an isolated area, so the workers had to buy their food from the

Chapter 7: Practices that Violate Human Dignity

company store, at very exorbitant prices. For Marx, this is where the exploitation lies. In his view, since the workers produced it, they should be free to taste the fruits of what they produced, both materially and financially.

After the failure of communism, should capitalism have been the goal for Eastern Europe and the Third World?

> "The answer is obviously complex. If by 'capitalism' is meant an economic system which recognizes the fundamental and positive role of business, the market, private property and the resulting responsibility for the means of production, as well as free human creativity in the economic sector, then the answer is certainly in the affirmative, even though it would perhaps be more appropriate to speak of a 'business economy', 'market economy' or simply 'free economy'. But if by "capitalism" is meant a system in which freedom in the economic sector is not circumscribed within a strong juridical framework which places it at the service of human freedom in its totality, and which sees it as a particular aspect of that freedom, the core of which is ethical and religious, then the reply is certainly negative.
>
> The Marxist solution has failed, but the realities of marginalization and exploitation remain in the world, especially the Third World, as does the reality of human alienation, especially in the more advanced countries. Against these phenomena the Church strongly raises

her voice. Vast multitudes are still living in conditions of great material and moral poverty.[8]

According to Saint Pope John Paul II,

"'Man is treated as an instrument of production [cf. Pope Pius XI, Encyclical *Quadragesimo Anno*: *AAS* 23 (1931), p. 221.],' whereas he–alone, independent of the work he does–ought to be treated as the effective subject of work and its true maker and creator. Precisely this reversal of order, whatever the program or name under which it occurs, should rightly be called 'capitalism' . . . . Everybody knows that capitalism has a definite historical meaning as a system, an economic and social system, opposed to 'socialism' or 'communism.' But in light of the analysis of the fundamental reality of the whole economic process–first and foremost of the production structure that work is–it should be recognized that the error of early capitalism can be repeated wherever people are treated on the same level as the whole complex of the material means of production, as an instrument and not in accordance with the true dignity of their work."[9]

---

[8] Ibid., §42.
[9] John Paul II, *Laborem Exercens*, §30.

Any labor that doesn't welcome the happiness and promotion of man's dignity should be eradicated. Such labor does not aim at uniting the human society, but rather leads to creating classes in it. As opined by the National Conference of Catholic Bishops,

"Some in our own community welcome the tradition's teaching on private property, the limits of the state, the advantages of free markets and the condemnation of communism, but resist the focus on the poor, the defense of labor unions, the recognition of the moral limits of markets and the responsibilities of government. Others welcome the teaching on the 'option for the poor,' the duties of government to protect the weak, the warnings against unbridled capitalism, but seem to ignore the centrality of family, the emphasis on economic initiative, and the warnings against the bureaucratic excesses of a 'social assistance' state. Our social tradition is a moral framework. . . It challenges both right and left, labor and management to focus on the dignity of the human person and the common good rather than their own political or economic interests."[10]

---

[10] National Conference of Catholic Bishops, A Decade after Economic Justice for All Continuing Principles, Changing Contest, New Challenges, (Washington, D.C.: USCCB, 1996), §2.

Therefore, we must redress any form of exploitation through labor. Human beings were created and placed in society to honor God and his gifts by using work as a means to support themselves, their families, and their society. In this endeavor, it would be meaningless if what humans created turned around to be against self and dignity.

Bonded Labor

In the 19th century, Asians were sent to labor through mortgaging of products to drug addicts in China. When scarcity of products occurs, people decided to be bonded to labor so as a means of survival. Bonded labor not only violates the dignity of man, but also enslaves man.

Bonded labor is a means of exploiting man through his labor. In this scenario, the money normally paid to the worker for that labor is, instead, diverted to a debt-holder as redemption of that debt. Unfortunately, the amount owed and the terms of repayment are such that the debt cannot be paid-off due to the lack of monetary resources at hand. It is the poor and the minority groups within society who become the victims of this kind of labor. The desperation of the laborer can be exploited by the *master* who wishes to coerce the debtor into signing an agreement which may be destructive to the dignity of the debtor.

With bonded labor, the freedom of man is denied, and he remains in the *custody* of his fellow man. Often, the laborer is not given a break or allowed to do certain things without the permission of the debt holder. His freedom is regulated until he satisfies the debt fully. In the meantime, the debt holder is often treating the debtor in such a way as to maximize the work he produces while, at the same time, prolonging the time it takes to satisfy the debt. One of the characteristics of being a human person is the ability to exercise one's free will by making decisions/choices concerning one's life. It is this ability that identifies one as a thinking rational human being. When one is controlled by another, without having first been granted the unencumbered free-will choice to do so by the debtor, the actions that result will never be original.

This type of labor has been rampant in Africa during the 17th century, continuing up to, and even beyond, the abolition of the slave trade in the 19th century. Africa is not, by far, the only continent to engage in this practice. Paraphrasing the words of Pope Francis, as long as the problems of the poor are not radically resolved by rejecting the absolute autonomy of markets, financial speculators, and the structural causes of inequality, no solution will be found to the world's problems or, for that matter, to any problems having to do with human dignity. Inequality is all too often the root of social ills.[11]

---

[11] Pope Francis, *Evangelii* Gaudium, §202.

Bonded labor, as well as any type of exploited labor, constitutes an attack on human dignity. It instrumentalizes and exploits the innate value of man created in the image and likeness of a Good and Loving God. Any exploitive system must be vigorously opposed. Pope Francis states,

> "Today, we also have to say 'thou shalt not' to an economy of exclusion and inequality. Such an economy kills. How can it be that it is not a news item when an elderly homeless person dies of exposure, but it is news when the stock market loses two points? This is a case of exclusion. Can we continue to stand by when food is thrown away while people are starving? This is a case of inequality. Today everything comes under the laws of competition and the survival of the fittest, where the powerful feed upon the powerless. As a consequence, masses of people find themselves excluded and marginalized: without work, without possibilities, without any means of escape."[12]

---

[12] Ibid., §53.

Chapter Eight

Different Stages in the Development of the Idea of Human Dignity

Man has lived in the world for many millennia. The rationality with which the Creator has endowed man has enabled him to form, over time, concepts relative to his surroundings, his fellow-men, and his own being. Thus, man progressively developed and expanded an understanding of the extraordinary uniqueness of each individual.

It was not difficult for each man to be convinced of his own dignity. In time, it became logically apparent that each man held the same view of himself. It was seen that this situation called for mutual recognition–this kind of conception made man not only able to form his own group or tribal community, but to deal with and negotiate with other groups and tribes encountered. This great issue of social complexity eventually birthed the notion of dignity in the human being.

The stages of development of the understanding of human dignity range from the natural approach of different philosophers such as Cicero (in particular) and Saints Ambrose, Augustine, and Bernard of Clairvaux. All helped to expand the concept with the *Christ-centered* thought, which was perfected by Saint Thomas Aquinas. Also, we shall consider the influence of Immanuel Kant on modern thought by relating human dignity to reason. Lastly, we will examine the influences on the idea of human dignity as it came to be used in the 1948 Universal Declaration of Human Rights. Some thought will be given to the unfortunate Mary Wollstonecraft, whose writings have become fashionable again under the influence of the modern feminist movement. For "to understand how human dignity is understood today, one needs to go back historically to the way the occidental world understood the concept."[1]

Cosmo-centric View

The naturalistic account tried to evaluate man's nature in the cosmos. What it means to have dignity in the cosmos was the center of all discussions. Plato (427-347 B.C.), the great philosopher, tried evaluating this notion of man's

---

[1] R.P. Horstmann, *Menschenwürde*, trans. Joachim Ritter and Karlfried Gründer (Hg.), Historisches Wörterbuch der Philosophie, Band 5, (Basel/Stuttgart: Schwabe & Co. AG, 1980), 1124-1127.

Chapter 8: Stages in the Dev. of the Idea of Human Dignity

having dignity, but he arrived at the Absolute Good while using political instances. For him, the dignity of man could be seen only at the political level when related to the Absolute Good. In his affirmation of Plato's view, Aristotle (384-322 B.C.) further explained the Platonic approach as a type of dignity that excludes both foreigners and slaves while benefiting only citizens of the state in a democratic government. This explanation frustrated any development of the concept of a universal human dignity. This notion of dignity in Aristotle is gotten from Latin, a meaning ranging from the Greek ἀξίωμα (*axioma* = axiom, in which one is thought worthy and so, esteem, reputation, rank) and ἀξία (*Axia* = the worth or value of a thing, or person, worth, rank) so systematically as in the Latin, *dignitas*.[2]

After the propositions of Plato and Aristotle came that of the Stoics whose philosophy differed yet again. They saw human dignity from the viewpoint of reason but not of legality within the State, thus relegating human dignity to the possession of reason. Man's possession of reason made him superior to all other creatures and, for them, that

---

[2] Aristotle, *Posterior Analytics*, trans. Hugh Tredennick and E. S. Forster, The Loeb Classical Library 391, William Heinemann, London 1960, I, VII (75a38-75b3), I,X (76b13-15); and *Nicomachean Ethics*, trans. H. Rackham, Loeb Classical Library, Vol.73, Harvard University Press, Cambridge 1990, IV,3 (1123a3425a31).

justified the attribution of *dignity* to man. This definition of man and his dignity recognized, for the first time, the universality of Human Dignity.

On this basis, we explore the notion of dignity in Marcus Tullius Cicero (106–43 B.C.). He was a Roman politician, lawyer, orator, and author. His work, *De officiis* (On Duties), expanded on the *dignitas hominis,* further arguing against the notions of Plato and Aristotle. Cicero affirmed the position of the Stoics. Man is not controlled by instinct like the beasts and other creatures, but instead by reason or intellect. It is thus that he can regulate his actions, which in turn establishes his Human Dignity. Cicero states:

> But it is essential to every inquiry about duty that we keep before our eyes how far superior man is by nature to cattle and other beasts: they have no thought except for sensual pleasure and this they are impelled by every instinct to seek, but man's mind is nurtured by study and meditation; he is always either investigating or doing, and he is captivated by the pleasure of seeing and hearing. Nay, even if a man is more than ordinarily inclined to sensual pleasures, provided, of course, that he be not quite on a level with the beasts of the field (for some people are men only in name, not in fact) . . . . From this we see that sensual pleasure is quite unworthy of the dignity of man [*dignam hominis*] and that we ought to despise it and cast it from us; but if

someone should be found who sets some value upon sensual gratification, he must keep strictly within the limits of moderate indulgence. One's physical comforts and wants, therefore, should be ordered according to the demands of health and strength, not according to the calls of pleasure. And if we will only bear in mind the superiority and dignity of our nature [*natura excellentia et dignitas*], we shall realize how wrong it is to abandon ourselves to excess and to live in luxury and voluptuousness, and how right it is to live in thrift, self-denial, simplicity, and sobriety.[3]

Mild amusement may be derived from Cicero's noble enunciation of these truths when we reflect on what history knows of his own generally very wealthy, though not often excessive, lifestyle. In this position taken by Cicero, the power of reasoning makes human dignity universal, contrary to the position of Plato and Aristotle, who made this dignity an attribute limited to those properly belonging in the society–a civic entitlement, so to speak. This reflects something of the earlier distinction made, when we differentiated between inherent dignity and that acquired

---

[3] Marcus T. Cicero, *De Officiis*, trans. Walter, Miller, vol. 21, (London: Harvard University Press, 1913/Reprint 1975), The Loeb Classical Library, 107–109.

in the State, due to status or position, taking for instance the Judges, Reverend Fathers, the Pope, etc.

Christo-centric View

This view aims to link this inherent value in man to God through His creation of man and the Incarnation of Christ. From the beginning of Christianity, it has been consistently taught to us, via the teachings of Jesus Christ, the reality of Fatherhood of God, and thus the brotherhood of Man.

The medieval era was characterized as the Age of Faith, made clear through the teachings of the Church. It was during this age that the Church was free to teach about God, the creation of man, and rights of this man who is created in the image and likeness of God. All questions of this time were answered in relation to God's teachings.

The Dominican Friar, Saint Thomas Aquinas (A.D. 1225-1274), the Angelic Doctor, Doctor of the Sacred Page, Scripture Professor, Theologian, Philosopher, Hymnist, and Mystic was the greatest medieval Christian writer. He addressed the issue of human dignity, giving it a meaningful definition by working from Sacred Scripture, the teachings of Saint Ambrose, Saint Augustine, and, closer to his time, Saint Bernard of Clairvaux. He also developed his theological thoughts under the influences of both Boethius and Cicero's classical account of personhood and dignity.

For Saint Thomas Aquinas, a person is a unique being with a rational nature that possesses autonomous importance. From this comes the understanding of the most important value in a human person—it is called *dignity*. Here, he never deviated from the definition of the Stoics and Cicero who tried giving distinct importance in society through the possession of reason. In his Theocentric era, Christian writers affirm that man is created in the image and likeness of God, and through the creation of man and the Incarnation of Christ, man is universally possessed of a dignity that is contrary to the poor restricted concept of Plato and Aristotle. This epoch, transforms the *Dignitas hominis* of Cicero starting from Sacred Scripture, then from the work of Saint Ambrose of Milan (A.D. 340-397), in which he coined the term, *dignitas conditione humana* (the dignity of human condition or creation).[4] This coinage can

---

[4] St. Ambrose, *De Dignitate Conditionis* Humanae, PL 17, 1015-1018; PL 40, 1213-1214 (exc.); PL 100, 565-568; cf. *Clavis Patristica Pseudegraphicum Medii Aevii IIB*, in: CCL, (Turnholt: Brepols, 1994), 683, No. 3008.

also be seen in Saint Bernard of Clairvaux[5] (A.D. 1090–1153) and in the work of Saint Thomas Aquinas, himself.[6]

It is pertinent to mention that the medieval era gave human dignity a Christo-centric consideration, which portrayed humans as rational beings endowed with dignity by the virtue of being created by the Divine. So, through our special creation we are equal and deserve respect, for we are dignified in God, and through the Incarnation of His Son, Jesus Christ.

Logo-centric View

This view linked itself with the humanism of the Italian Renaissance which was based on the Christo-centric view. In his famous *Oratio de dignitate hominis*, Pico Della Mirandola (1463-1494), posited man as a being with free will who freely chooses how to live his life without any limitation of any kind. For him, "men and women are hybrid beings who freely choose the blueprint of their exis-

---

[5] Ibid., PL 184, 485-508.

[6] St. Thomas Aquinas, *The Summa Theologica of St. Thomas Aquinas*, II-II, QQ, CI-CXL, Literally translated by Fathers of the English Dominican Province, Second and Revised Edition, (London: Burns Oates & Washbourne Ltd, 1922), 10-12, 98.

tence."⁷ He stood firm with the two reoccurring terms in our previous discussion on man and his dignity, which are rationality and creation in the image and likeness of God.

Thomas Hobbes (1588-1679) was an English political philosopher, whose position on the dignity of man reverted, in essence, to that of Aristotle, which was based on the position of one in the society as in the Cosmo-centric view. He only recognizes dignity in those who occupy offices of command, public employment, and even names and titles as indicated by the commonwealth. This states that the worth and value of man lies in his state in society; this very worth and value can be called the dignity of man. One secures dignity only from his status in society. It was this that provoked a reflexive question from the dissertation of Augustine Anthony Regensburg on the human dignity from the beginning of life. It goes thus: "If the value bestowed on human persons rests on the commonwealth, who becomes the arbitrator when commonwealth itself

---

⁷ "Of the Dignity of Man: Oration of Giovanni Pico Della Mirandola, Count of Concordia," trans. Elizabeth Livermore Forbes, *Journal of the History of Ideas* 3 (1942), 347–354. Reprinted as: "Oration on the Dignity of Man," translated by Elizabeth Livermore` Forbes, *The Renaissance Philosophy of Man*, ed. by Ernst Cassirer, Paul Oskar Kristeller, John Herman Randall, Jr. (Chicago: University of Chicago Press, 1948), 223–254.

does not respect the dignity of the person?"[8] Good question!

A German natural law Philosopher, Samuel Freiherr von Pufendorf (1632-1694), tried putting Thomas Hobbes on the right track by attributing human dignity to the social and political status of man within society. Pufendorff gave *dignitas* a nice definition as "a price and honor given in both political and social sense."[9] He considers man's dignity as rooted in the willpower and rationality of man, which enables him to contemplate things and decide to follow either the good or the bad. "Now the dignity of man far outshines that of beasts by virtue of the fact that he has been endowed with a most exalted soul, which, by its highly developed understanding, can examine into things and judge between them, and by its remarkable deftness, can embrace or reject them."[10] For Pufendorf, since all man, by

---

[8] Augustine Anthony Regensburg, The Human Dignity From the Beginning of Life: German and Indian Moral Theological Perspectives In an Attempt at Dialogue With Hinduism, Doctoral dissertation, (University of Regensburg, 2014), https://epub.uni-regensburg.de/30660/1/Dissertation-ANTHONY.pdf, 25.

[9] Samuel Pufendorf, *De* Jure *Naturae et Gentium Libri Octo: The Translation Of The Edition Of 1688*, Classics of International Law, Issue 17, vol. 1, trans. C.H. Oldfather, William A. Oldfather, (New York, Oceana Publications, 1964), 8, 4 §13.

[10] Ibid., 1, 3 § 1.

the virtue of possessing rationality, are equal regardless of their social or political status, they ought to be respected by the other. For man should be respected for who he is. However, respect of the other person applies only when one first respects himself. Recognizing the dignity in oneself enables us to see it in the other as possessing the same features and attributes as all human beings classified in one group. Freedom and rationality are the key concepts that make up the definition of dignitas by Pufendorf.

The above provided a steppingstone to the assertion of Immanuel Kant (1724-1804), a German philosopher. For Kant, dignity is that which is seen in all men due to the very fact that they possess rationality. It is this rational nature of man that made him independent. According to Kant, "In the kingdom of ends, everything has either value or dignity. Whatever has a value can be replaced by something else which is equivalent; whatever, on the other hand, is above all value, and therefore admits of no equivalent, has a dignity."[11] This distinctive integration of the two concepts, i.e. dignity and price, in human nature are characteristic of Kant. For him, there is a clear distinction between the two words dignity (Würde) and price (Wert). To Kant, Dignity is that worth which is intrinsic in human and also a moral

---

[11] Immanuel Kant, *Fundamental* Principles *of the Metaphysics of Morals*, trans. Thomas Kingsmill Abbott, (Rockville: Arc Manor Publishing, 2008), 52.

value given to man, while price is that value in man, given to him by society. Here, in so far as man is rationally independent, he has inherent dignity, while the price is that type of dignity given by the society, such as any public offices which man occupies. Kant also spoke of man as being an end in himself, who should not be instrumentalized by the other in the society. Kant said "But man regarded as a person, that is, as the subject of a morally practical reason, is exalted above any price; for as a person (*homo noumenon*) he is not to be valued merely as a means to the ends of others or even to his own ends, but as an end in himself, that is, he possesses a dignity (an absolute inner worth) by which he exacts respect for himself from all other rational beings in the world. He can measure himself with every other being of his kind and value himself on a footing of equality with them."[12]

Man is to be regarded as an end, and not a means to an end. When one is seen as a means to the actualization of a particular thing, he is reduced to the level of a thing or an object. Rather, man should be seen as a subject and not an object.

These assertions of Kant are centered on rationality and autonomy, which give man his dignity and, for the very fact

---

[12] Immanuel Kant, *The Metaphysics of* Morals, trans. Mary Gregor, (Cambridge: Cambridge University Press, 1991), 230.

that man is endowed with this rational nature, he is to be respected by the other.

Polis-centric View

The polis-centric view centers on Mary Wollstonecraft's view of dignity and also the influences on the idea of human dignity as it came to be used in the 1948 Universal Declaration of Human Rights. All the developments above drew the attention of Mary Wollstonecraft in the so-called postmodern era, leading her to solicit for a better society where the dignity of all humans could be recognized, regardless of their sex, taking the view that all are one in the human family and should not be segregated. For her, the fact that man, in general (which *de facto* includes women), possesses the rationality mentioned by Kant, women, who are also rational beings, should be accorded the same dignity.[13] In the "Vindication of the Rights of Men" in the year (1790), and also the "Vindication of the Rights of Woman" in the year (1792), she solicits for the social inclusion of *women* and *common men* in society. She adopted a view on dignity which led to the coinage of the

---

[13] Mary Wollstonecraft, *Political writings: A vindication of the Rightsof Men, a Vindication of the Rights of Woman*, An Historical and Moral View of the French Revolution. Ed. Janet Todd. Oxford: Oxford UP, 1994.

phrases: the *native dignity of man*; the *dignity of character*, or the *dignity of virtue* instead of following the phrase, human dignity, as used in the previous development. This helped her create awareness on the realization of the native dignity of every man in society in order to help in the respect of one's dignity despite his status, state, or sex in the society.[14]

The Universal Declaration of Human Rights enacted by the UN Charter in San Francisco on June 26, 1945,[15] is found in different countries of the world and is at least in thirty-seven National Constitutions. The declaration of these rights follows the realization of the fact that man's dignity is inherent and ought not to be violated. It is clear that the enactment of these rights of man originates from the words of Sacred Scripture. Through Scripture we come to understand that the dignity of man is rooted in God. More precisely, it is through his creation in the image and likeness of his Creator and also the Natural Law from whence other laws in the universe take their being. These two sources, seen in the human rights declared by the U.N. charter, gave man equal rights in any society in which they

---

[14] Ibid.

[15] United Nations Organization, "Relevant Provisions of the United Nations Charter, 1945," ed. Ian Brownlie, Guy S. Goodwin-Gill, *Basic Documents on Human Rights*, (New York: Oxford University Press, 2010), 1–13, 3.

found themselves, as indicated in the German Constitution of May 23, 1949. In the Constitution it says, "Human Dignity is inviolable. To respect and protect it shall be the duty of all state authority."[16]

The U.N. Charter has a very nice vision of the redemption of man from the hands of segregation of any kind, sex abuse, child abuse, human trafficking, and any other abuses. Anything relating to the instrumentalization and objectification of man is rejected by this Charter: "to reaffirm faith in fundamental human rights, in the dignity and worth of the human person, in the equal rights of men and women and of nations large and small."[17]

This voyage toward the redemption of man from both social and political inequalities, leading to the universal equality granted by the Divine, can be completed. As stated in the Preambles of International Covenant on Economic, Social and Cultural Rights, 1966, and International Covenant on Civil and Political Rights, 1966, "These [human] rights derive from the inherent dignity of the human person."[18]

---

[16] German Federal Ministry of Justice, "German Federal Republic. Basic Law...," 361. Hailer/Ritschl, "The General Notion of Human Dignity...," 101.

[17] U.N., "Relevant Provisions of the United Nations Charter, 1945," 1.

[18] United Nations General Assembly, "International Covenant on Economic, Social and Cultural Rights, 1966," ed.

The emergence of human rights came as a rescue mission to save man from exploitation and dehumanization. From whom did they need to be rescued? Unfortunately, because we live in fallen creation, some people have come to believe that some people are *more unique* (or "more equal" as George Orwell described it the 1945 novella, *Animal Farm*) and, therefore, more valuable. These are the societal groups that create the need for rescue. Society must put a stop to the past phenomenological abnormalities caused by man himself, born of ignorance of the inestimable worth of every man, be he rich or poor, educated or uneducated, this color or that color, and the list could go on.

That the human rights movement was so decisive should be seen as reflection of the positive force of the Christo-centric view and of man's recoiling in horror at seeing and experiencing such horrendous death and suffering perpetrated by: 1) the calamitous excesses of World Wars I and II; 2) totalitarian Communist; 3) The National Socialist Nazi's, and other Fascist regimes. Therefore, it is of value to welcome and acknowledge this idealistic mission that called, and continues to call, to our consciousness the rights we have as humans, and to totally reject any violation of the dignity of the other.

Ian Brownlie and Guy S. Goodwin-Gill, *Basic* Documents *on Human Rights*, 348–357, 358–374.

Chapter Nine

The Church's Stand on Human Dignity

Sacred Scripture provides the kernel of the Catholic view of the human person. It establishes the dignity of the human person and the intrinsic value of human life.[1]

The Church has had her teaching rooted in human dignity from her very beginnings. It is implicit in the Revelation of Sacred Scripture, starting from the Old Testament (OT) and continuing in the New Testament (NT). The creation of man in the image and likeness of God is a fundamental theological teaching of God through the Scriptures from the very beginning, Genesis 1:26-27 to be exact. In the OT, man is shown as a being with the unique dignity that he is created by the Divine in His own image and likeness, "For the Old Testament, this concept of 'image of God' is not merely a religious overlay on natural humanity, but something fundamental to authentic

---

[1] Thomas Srampickal, "The Catholic View of Human Life and Abortion," ed. Dr. Joseph Alencherry and Dr. Scaria Kanniyakonil, (Thuruthy, Kerala, India: CANA Publications, 2005), 82.

humanity."² In taking up the question of what the *Imago Dei* means for human personhood, we address an issue that touches virtually every other tenet of Christian belief. It is not too much to say that the core of the theological curriculum itself is contained in the Doctrine of the Imago Dei.³

In the New Testament, man can be seen as a being with dignity through the Incarnation of the Son of God, who has become Man, truly sharing our very being. The NT admits that every human being has the possibility of becoming a child of God.⁴ The deepest significance of being made in the image of God is the idea of being children of God.

During the medieval era, when the Church's influence was at its peak–the Age of Faith–there came the reflection and studies of the Church Fathers. They wrote in defense of the teachings of the Church, making reference to philosophical questions and teachings of the ancient era so as to give reasoned theological and convincing answers to questions that preoccupied their epoch. The Church Fathers contemplated how creation in the image of God contri-

---

[2] Federation of Asian Bishops Conference (FABC): Office of Theological Concerns, "Respect for Life in the Context of Asia," Paper #120, (Hong Kong: *Federation of Asian Bishops Conference*, 2007), 33.

[3] Ray S. Anderson, *On Being Human: Essays in Theological Anthropology*, (Grand Rapids: Wm. B. Eerdmans Publishing Company, 1982), 70.

[4] FABC, "Respect for Life in the Context of Asia," 39.

buted to the emergence of dignity; how man possesses this dignity through his creation by the Infinite and his sharing in the Incarnation of the Son of God.

Of all these defenders of the Catholic Faith, St. Irenaeus (A.D. 130-202), Bishop of Lyons, was the first to create a stir in the Church and in society due to his famous dictum, which goes thus; "*Gloria enim Dei vivens homo, vita autem hominis visio Dei,*" which means, "For the glory of God, is a living man; and the life of man consists in beholding God."[5] It was against this backdrop that Irenaeus started to look deeply into the nature of man as a being with dignity. His view also linked to the New Testament, specifically the Incarnation of the Son of God. The incarnation was the foundation of Irenaeus' assertion though he didn't negate the account of the OT. For Irenaeus, in the creation of man by God, man was said to be made in the image of God (*imago Dei*). But it was not made clear to our understanding precisely how this was so.

However, the coming of the Son of God in human form not only demonstrated the love of the Father for man, His creation, but it also showed the resemblance of humanity to God, for the Word which is God became truly man and

---

[5] Irenaeus Lugdunensis, "Adversus Haereses," IV, 20, 7, ed. Philip Schaff, *Ante-Nicene Fathers*, vol. 1, Christian Classics Ethereal Library, (Grand Rapids: Wm. B. Eerdmans Publishing Company, 2001), 819.

dwelt among men. It was made clear to us that we are indeed created in the image and likeness of God. Let us consider his writing, as seen above. Saint Irenaeus wrote thus;

> "And then, again, this Word was manifested when the Word of God was made man, assimilating Himself to man, and man to Himself, so that by means of his resemblance to the Son, man might become precious to the Father. For in times long past, it was said that man was created after the image of God, but it was not [actually] shown; for the Word was as yet invisible, after whose image man was created, Wherefore also he did easily lose the similitude. When, however, the Word of God became flesh, He confirmed both these: for He both showed forth the image truly since He became Himself what His image was; and He re-established the similitude after a sure manner, by assimilating man to the invisible Father through means of the visible Word."[6]

In all this, Irenaeus did not negate the concept of the dignity of man being rooted in reason and freedom.[7]

---

[6] Ibid., 914.

[7] Human Dignity in Indian Secularism, *Human Dignity in Indian Secularism and in Christianity*, (Bangalore, India: Claretian Publications, 2007), 273.

In his relationship with the Divine, man, through creation, was made to have a common association with the others in society, in unity, and in love. Love is the foundation of the creation of man in God's very image and likeness. Saint John tells us that God is Love (1 Jn 4:16).[8] It was this likeness of man to God that idealized the relationship between him and the man, who was created immortal, but chose mortality when he chose disobedience.

The kind of association that ought to exist among men to help one another inspired Tertullian's (A.D. 155-240) illustration using the Trinity as an example of the ideal. Tertullian, one of the great Fathers of the Church, in his doctrine of the Trinity which he designated as *Persona*, said:

> "Just as one cannot think of the 'person' of Father or Son or Spirit without the others, so one cannot think of the human person without others, as if human personhood were prior to and independent of community. Human persons too are persons-in-relation. And it is in

---

[8] Allen Verhey, *Reading the Bible in the Strange World of Medicine*, (Grand Rapids: Wm. B. Eerdmans Publishing Company, 2003), 93. For a further work on the Trinity and the notion of persons, see Alan J. Torrance, *Persons in Communion. An Essay on Trinitarian Description and Human Participation*, (Edinburgh: T&T Clark, 1996).

and as bodily beings that we are in relation to others and to God."⁹

Saint Augustine (A.D. 354–430), the great Doctor of the Church, developed Tertullian's illustration of the common association between man and his fellows in society, together with God. Augustine, believing in the power of the rationality in man, affirmed the very fact that the Divine image in us orients our spirits towards contemplative union with God.¹⁰ It was here that Augustine drew his assertion that affirmed that of Tertullian when he talked about the nature of the Trinity in man.

For Augustine, the nature of the triune God in man is rooted in his rationality, which includes memory, understanding, and will (love). This tripartite nature of the rationality of man he traced back to the Triune God as he rightly argued:

---

⁹ Tertullian,*Against Praxeas*.Translated by Peter Holmes. From Ante-Nicene Fathers, Vol. 3. Edited by Alexander Roberts, James Donaldson, and A. Cleveland Coxe. (Buffalo, NY: Christian Literature Publishing Co., 1885.) Revised and edited for New Advent by Kevin Knight. <http://www.newadvent.org/fathers/0317.htm>.

¹⁰ De Trinitate 14:15. See Augustine, De Trinitate, ed. W. J. Mountain and F. Glorie, CCL 50A, (Brepols Editores Pontificii, Turnholt 1968); Cf. Felix M. Podimattam, *Why be Moral?*, (Media House, 2005), 57.

"For if we refer ourselves to the inner memory of the mind by which it remembers itself, and to the inner understanding by which it understands itself, and to the inner will by which it loves itself, where these three always are together, and always have been together since they began to be at all, whether they were being thought of or not; the image of this trinity will indeed appear to pertain even to the memory alone; but because in this case, a word cannot be without a thought (for we think all that we say, even if it be said by that inner word which belongs to no separate language), this image is rather to be discerned in these three things, viz. memory, intelligence, will (De Trinitate 14.7.10)."[11]

---

[11] De Trinitate; 14.7.10. Augustine, "The Trinity," ed. John E. Rotelle, *The Works of Saint Augustine. A Translation for the 21st Century*, vol. 1, 5, (Brooklyn: New City Press, New York, 1991. The Latin text reads, «Nam si nos referamus ad interiorem mentis memoriam qua sui meminit, et interiorem intellegentiam qua se intellegit et interiorem uoluntatem qua se diligit, ubi haec tria simul sunt et simul semper fuerunt ex quo esse coeperunt siue cogitarentur siue non cogitarentur, uidebitur quidem imago illius trinitatis et ad solam memoriam pertinere. Sed quia ibi uerbum esse sine cogitatione non potest (cogitamus enim omne quod dicimus etiam illo interiore uerbo quod ad nullius gentis pertinet linguam), in tribus potius illis imago ista cognoscitur, memoria scilicet, intellegentia, uoluntate.» Cf. Sheri Katz,

To clarify further, Saint Thomas Aquinas, the Angelic Doctor of the Church, quoted Augustine in his writing, "Augustine says (Gn ad lit. vi, 12): 'Man's excellence consists in the fact that God made him to his own image by giving him an intellectual soul.'"[12] He went further to say that this special excellence consists in having dominion over one's own activity,[13] that is, since we have resemblance with God through domination of our decisions upon which our actions follow. Finally, he acclaimed that sin is the only thing that can deface this resemblance with the Divine. To sin is to fall off the track of good reasoning.

There are other authorities in the Church we could have referred to, but the strong outline of the Church's teaching has been presented. Both *Catechismus Romanus* (The Roman Catechism), introduced by Pius V (1504-1572) in 1556, and the *Catechism of the Catholic Church*, introduced by Saint Pope John Paul II in 1994, made significant contributions to the rich development of the concept of

---

"Person," ed. Allan D. Fitzgerald, *Augustine Through the Ages. An Encyclopedia*, (Grand Rapids: Wm. B. Eerdmans Publishing Co., 1999), 647-650.

[12] St. Thomas Aquinas, *The Summa Theologiae*, trans. Fathers of the English Dominican Province, Second and revised edition (London: Burns Oates and Washbourne, 1922), I, q. 93, a. 2 [contrary].

[13] Ibid., I, q. 93, a. 7, [answer].

human dignity.[14] Through documented works and teachings of the Catholic Church following the Church Fathers, until today, the idea of human dignity has been made to penetrate deep into our societies, calling to the consciousness of man the truth about his freedom and equality with the others.

Pope Leo XIII, in the year 1891 wrote his encyclical known as *Rerum Novarum* (Concerning New Issues The Condition of Labor). In society, the condition of labor was indeed being exploited due to the industrial revolution and the demands and possibilities of mechanized production. This led to the frequent treatment of workers as though they existed without dignity and were not human. The Church, in her motherly affection, moved further in soliciting for a fair treatment of these workers through the realization of their rights, through the organizing of labor unions, and also assuring all the right to own properties. Pope Leo writes, "Private ownership, as we have seen, is the natural right of man, and to exercise that right, especially as members of society, is not only lawful but absolutely necessary. 'It is lawful,' says St. Thomas Aquinas, 'for a man to

---

[14] Mathew Illathuparampil, "Promotion of Life. Claims on Economic Welfare," ed. Baiju Julian and Hormis Mynatty, *Catholic Contributions to Bioethics: Reflections on Evangelium Vitae*, (Bangalore: Asian Trading Corp., 2007), 97-98.

hold private property; and it is also necessary for the carrying on of human existence.'"¹⁵

In this way, Pope Leo XIII rebutted the swelling tide of Socialism and its successor, Communism. It was because of this growing tide that Pope Leo XIII sought to use human dignity as a yardstick, or standard of judgment, of the different sectors in the society, be it political, social, or economic structures. He said,

> "Let the working man and the employer make free agreements, and in particular let them agree freely as to the wages; nevertheless, there underlies a dictate of natural justice more imperious and ancient than any bargain between man and man, namely, that wages ought not to be insufficient to support a frugal and well-behaved wage-earner. If through necessity or fear of a worse evil, the workmen accept harder conditions because an employer or contractor will afford him no better, he is made the victim of force and injustice."¹⁶

This would make man an end and not a means to an end.

---

¹⁵ Pope Leo XIII, "Rerum Novarum. Encyclical of Pope Leo XIII on Capital and Labor May 15, 1891," ed. Claudia Carlen, *The Papal Encyclicals*, vol. 2, 1878-1903, (Wilmington: Consortium Books, McGrath Publishing Company, 1981), 22.

¹⁶ Ibid., 45.

Chapter 9: The Church's Stand on Human Dignity   135

In 1931, Pius XI (1857-1939) issued the encyclical *Quadragesimo Anno* (in the Fortieth Year–The Reconstruction of the Social Order), which came in the wake of the Great Depression in both the Capitalist and Communist societies. The Depression had devastated their social fabric and the dignity of the common man. Pope Pius XI, forty years after *Rerum Novarum*, addressed the resultant social problems existing in society by first pleading for an appropriate restructuring of government for the betterment of the masses and to uphold their dignity; secondly, he went further to consider implications of the idea of the ownership of private properties. He said that it is not so much a matter of the owning of private properties that are of concern, but the morality of the particular use of these private properties for the common good of the society.

In 1961, Saint Pope John XXIII wrote the Encyclical *Mater et Magistra*,[17] which means, (Mother and Teacher). Here, he sought a better society through the full participation of every individual, both in social and political positions. This encyclical showed the Church's position as a mother and a teacher, and it described the efforts of the Church in the realization of the dignity of humans by

---

[17] Pope John XXIII. "Encyclical Letter. Mater et Magistra," ed. Michael Walsh and Brian Davies, *Proclaiming Justice and Peace. Documents from John XXIII to John Paul II*, (Mystic: Twenty-third Publications, 1985), 1-44.

giving everyone the chance to participate in social and political offices. He used this encyclical to celebrate the 70th anniversary of *Rerum Novarum*.[18]

In 1963, Saint Pope John XXIII issued *Pacem in Terris* (Peace on Earth),[19] which was addressed to all men of goodwill, unlike the other writing of his which were addressed in the normal manner, i.e., to the Church. The situation that sparked this encyclical was the threat of missiles and nuclear warfare, which raised the specter of countries eradicating one another through wars. Countries were showing how powerful they were by using other countries as ground for weapons testing, thus paving the way for destruction rather than development. All was to the detriment of the poor in the respective societies. *Pacem in Terris* stated that,

> "Any well-regulated and productive association of men in society demands the acceptance of one fundamental principle: that each individual man is truly a person. His is a nature that is, endowed with intelligence and free will. As such, he has rights and duties, which together flow as a direct consequence of his nature. These rights and duties are universal and inviolable,

---

[18] Leo XIII, "Rerum Novarum. Encyclical of Pope Leo XIII on Capital and Labor May 15, 1891," 241-262.

[19] John XXIII, *Pacem in* Terris, §45-76.

and therefore, altogether inalienable. When, furthermore, we consider man's personal dignity from the standpoint of Divine Revelation, inevitably our estimate of it is incomparably increased. Men have been ransomed by the blood of Jesus Christ. Grace has made them sons and friends of God, and heirs to eternal glory (PT 9-10)."[20]

Saint Pope John XXIII went further in pleading for social and economic rights, not just political and legal rights, through a communal life that upholds the dignity of all. He went further to call for a national unity where a state can help the other in the achievement of pressing needs.

In 1965, *Gaudium et Spes* (Joy and Hope), the Pastoral Constitution on the Church in the Modern World,[21] The Second Vatican Council was on the look-out for a way to make clear the role of the Church in the world. For there exist diverse ideologies in the world that threaten the dignity of man. The document went further to state that the idea of human dignity can be made clear and defended only

---

[20] Ibid., 49.

[21] Second Vatican Ecumenical Council, "Pastoral Constitution on the Church in the Modern World. Gaudium et Spes," ed. Walter, M. Abbot, *The Documents of Vatican II. All Sixteen Official Texts Promulgated by the Ecumenical Council 1963-1965*, trans. Joseph Gallagher (London: Geoffrey Chapman, 1967), 199-308.

if we recognize that human institutions and human persons are not static but develop and change over the course of history. Human dignity is presented positively as involving the right to share in the decisions that structure political, social, and economic life.

In *Gaudium et Spes*, it stated that the dignity of man lies in his relationship with the Creator. Therefore, our being with dignity lies in communion with God, which is our call. At the mention of man, our attention should go to the intrinsic worth of man, which makes him human and thus should not be violated: "there is a growing awareness of the exalted dignity proper to the human person since he and his rights and duties are universal and inviolable."[22]

Lastly, in *Gaudium et Spes*, the Church proclaims her stand on the dignity of man, standing by the Gospel and, with no qualm of any kind, declares,

> The Church can anchor the dignity of human nature against all tides of opinion, for example, those which undervalue the human body or idolize it. By no human law can the personal dignity and liberty of man be so aptly safeguarded as by the Gospel of Christ which has been entrusted to the Church. For this Gospel announces and proclaims the freedom of the sons of God, and repudiates all the bondage, which ultimately

---

[22] Gaudium et Spes, §26.

results from sin. (cf. Rom 8:14–17). The Gospel has a sacred reverence for the dignity of conscience and its freedom of choice. . . .Therefore, by virtue of the Gospel committed to her, the Church proclaims the rights of man.[23]

In 1967, Saint Pope Paul VI wrote *Populorum Progressio* (The Development of Peoples)[24] as a response to global poverty and hunger. People were suffering, and migration became the talk of the day. People moved from their homes in search of greener pastures, and at the risk of becoming the minority groups in the new society (the poor), since all the sectors in different societies favor select group of persons rather than all, making the distribution of goods and services one-sided. The encyclical pleaded for an "integral development" to help in the promotion of the dignity of man. Due to the situation, it saw a need for restructuring all aspects of life within each society in order to help everyone. He argued that this reform should be carried out in all the institutions of the society, be it political, social, or economic.

---

[23] Ibid., §41.

[24] Pope Paul VI, "Encyclical Letter. Populorum Progressio," ed. Michael Walsh and Brian Davies, *Proclaiming Justice and Peace. Documents from John XXIII to John Paul II*, (Mystic: Twenty-third Publications, 1985), 141-164.

With the publication of the Apostolic Letter *Octogesima Adveniens* (written on the eightieth anniversary of *Rerum Novarum*), Saint Pope Paul VI in 1971 issued a *call to action* concerning achievement of an increase in social justice and peace in the world. There was talk of increased exploitation of the aged, the handicapped, women, and children as a result of urbanization. The idea of urbanization had become a fashionable topic. The view had been presented to the Church that the phenomenon impoverished a great number of people due to the state of society when people were ignored and neglected for the sake of urbanization. By writing *Octogesima Adveniens,* the Pope sought to give a theological explanation of the situation by using faith, showing how it affects the dignity of humans, most especially those neglected and exploited.

Still on the matters of negligence and exploitation of man, in the year 1981, Saint Pope John Paul II issued his encyclical *Laborem Exercens* (Through Work), to redirect the notion of seeing others as a means to an end instead of an end themselves. Some employers valued the production that came from their workers more than the workers themselves. It was indeed exploiting, and some organizations saw huge economic benefits by shifting to the use of technologies in total replacement of their workers, thereby creating a high rate of unemployment. Saint Pope John Paul II sought to emphasize the prior rights of labor over capital. For in labor, the dignity of man is demonstrated.

Work exists due to the rationality of man who developed it to help his fellow man. Therefore, man should be seen as a subject, not as an object or instrument through which an end is achieved. Lastly, he called for the respect of human dignity during labor.

Sollicitudo Rei Socialis (On Social Concerns) was promulgated by Saint Pope John Paul II in 1987. Using the occasion of the twentieth anniversary of *Populorum Progressio*, the Pope looked deeper at the issues of development in both developed and underdeveloped countries. The question of standardizing the world economy became an issue in this epoch, and John Paul II used this encyclical to advise for the advancement of human solidarity, and for a deeper reflection on the idea of human dignity. That is where true development lies. There is no authentic development if there is no recognition of human dignity and solidarity among all in man's societies.

In the 1988 Post-Synodal Apostolic Exhortation *Christifideles Laici* (Christ's Lay Faithful),[25] John Paul II examined the idea of inequality among humans, more especially between the sexes. He used this Apostolic Exhortation as a way of touching on the rate of violation of human dignity existing in the world. He pleaded for a way

---

[25] John Paul II, Post-Synodal Apostolic Exhortation *Christifideles Laici*, (Vatican City: Libreria Editrice Vaticana, 1988).

of respecting the human person and his worth as a human person.

This exhortation talked about the equality of all humans, regardless of their race, color, or sex. He postulated that neither masculinity nor femininity makes a difference in the personhood of man; though their function in the society may differ, they still share in the same dignity as all humans created in the image and likeness of God. He wrote,

> "The condition that will assure the rightful presence of woman in the Church and in society is a more penetrating and accurate consideration of the anthropological foundation for masculinity and femininity with the intent of clarifying woman's personal identity in relation to man, that is, a diversity yet mutual complementarity, not only as it concerns roles to be held and functions to be performed, but also, and more deeply, as it concerns her make-up and meaning as a person."[26]

He made it clear that the Church's stand on the dignity of the human person is "to rediscover and make others rediscover the inviolable dignity of every human person."[26] Finally, he asserted that the dignity of man is inherent, and it can never be eradicated by any person or power.

---

[26] Ibid., §50.

In 1991, during the one-hundredth anniversary of *Rerum Novarum*, John Paul II wrote the encyclical *Centesimus Annus* (The One-Hundredth Year). The encyclical addressed the rise of atheism, new ideologies, and great changes in both political and economic powers, all of which posed a threat to human dignity. He acknowledged the dignity of the human person insofar as he is a person. He went further, acclaiming the source of this dignity, which he found in God. John Paul II said, "The human person receives from God its essential dignity and with it the capacity to transcend every social order so as to move towards truth and goodness."[27] He also affirmed the inviolability of human dignity since it comes from God. Certain human rights were laid bare in his work. He writes,

> "Among the most important of these rights, mention must be made of the right to life, an integral part of which is the right of the child to develop in the mother's womb from the moment of conception; the right to live in a united family and in a moral environment conducive to the growth of the child's personality; the right to develop one's intelligence and freedom in seeking and knowing the truth; the right to share in the work which makes wise use of the earth's material resources, and to derive from that work the means to support oneself and

---

[27] John Paul II, Centesimus *Annus*, §38.

one's dependents; and the right freely to establish a family, to have and to rear children through the responsible exercise of one's sexuality (*Centesimus Annus* §47; cf. Com. 155)."[28]

Recognizing the Church's stand on human dignity and the freedom of man, as stated in *Centesimus Annus*, John Paul II said; "Furthermore, in constantly reaffirming the transcendent dignity of the person, the Church's method is always that of respect for freedom."[29]

The third encyclical of Pope Benedict XVI was *Caritas in Veritate* (Charity in Truth), promulgated in 2009.[30] Benedict XVI was prompted to issue his encyclical following the decline of the world economy in the year

---

[28] cf. Arokiasamy Soosai S.J., "Human Dignity and Human Rights in the Catholic Social Teaching in Relation to the Church in India," a paper presented at: National Seminar on the *Compendium of the Social Doctrine of the Church*. This seminar was held from March 24-26, 2006 in Mumbai. It was organized by the Catholic Bishops Conference of India. 12; The text of Soosai's presentation can be read here: "Human Dignity," *Wisdom in Dialogue*, https://wisdomindialogue.blogspot.com/2008/04/human-dignity.html, April 8, 2008.

[29] John Paul II, Centesimus *Annus,* §46.

[30] Benedict XVI, Caritas *in Veritate*, §75.

2008.[31] He wrote it in order to lay emphasis on how the situation affected both human dignity and the society at large. For Benedict XVI, human dignity has its roots in the creation of man in God's image and likeness. The meaning of the dignity of man can be found in his creation by the Divine. He went further to state that since man exists and transcends all norms and laws of the society due to his inherent dignity, both the ethics of life and social ethics should be seen from the same angle as needed for the promotion of human dignity. He stood against some new inventions of science, more especially in the area of medicine dealing with human life, such as: "In vitro fertilization, embryo research, the possibility of manufacturing clones and human hybrids . . . [including also] the tragic and widespread scourge of abortion . . . [and] the systematic eugenic programming of births . . . and a pro-euthanasia mindset" (*Caritas in Veritate* §75).

Pope Francis's first encyclical, entitled *Lumen Fidei* (The Light of Faith), was published less than four months after his election to the papacy in the year 2013. It dealt with the examination of the Christian faith, owing to the occasion of the "Year of Faith," which had been declared by

---

[31] Robert Moynihan, "Caritas in Veritate," ed. Michael L. Coulter, Richard S. Myers, and Joseph A. Varacalli, *Encyclopedia of Catholic Social Thought, Social Science, and Social Policy*, vol. 3 (Supplement), (Lanham: Scarecrow Press, 2012), 41.

Pope Benedict XVI. In his second encyclical, entitled *Laudato Si* (Praise Be to You), Pope Francis tackled the phenomenological occurrences in society, such as environmental degradation, global warming, and irresponsible development. For him, there is a shift from the Theocentric idea of viewing things in the universe, to anthropocentric ideas. He said this because of the way we talk about man as if he is the creator of all things that are, thereby considering other living things as non-living things. Going further, he said the domination of man must not be seen from the extent of making man the creator of all the beings in the world, rather as a being among the family of all things that exist in the society. The lengthy encyclical proved very controversial owing to its heavy environmental rather than religious preoccupation.

With all those explicated above, one will realize that the Catholic Church has been adamant, from current times all the way back to ancient times, about the dignity of the human person. There are also many facts, as taught in the *Catechism of the Catholic Church,* about human dignity which have been compiled by the Church to educate her children about the preciousness of the human life–of every individual who is made in the image of the invisible God.

Chapter 10

Africa: Human Dignity at Risk

We have examined quite thoroughly the issues surrounding human dignity at the theoretical level. Yet something is lacking. We need to consider the complexity of the issues when operating in the real world.

Perhaps no other location so thoroughly meets the needs of the topic at hand as does Africa. Within this continent there exist: 1) a diverse population of 1.216 billion people; 2) a multiplicity of independent countries, and; 3) a multitude of varied customs and usages. Africa is, in effect, a laboratory *par excellence* for examining human dignity as it strives for recognition.

In Africa, we discover that we have an enormous history of political life and cultures–often strong for centuries, of diverse religions (mostly pagan)–and of varying attitudes toward human dignity right up to the present day. This work seeks to bare the facts relating to human dignity in Africa, both past and present. We shall find that Africa has played, and still plays, a sad but important role in the world's history of human dignity.

Africa, the second largest of the continents, is rich in culture and full of peoples of great abilities. The peoples of Africa have contributed immensely to the architectural heritage of the world. In natural resources and wildlife, Africa is beyond compare.

It is perhaps surprising then that, in the annals of world history, there are not more African citizens in the record. When we go back to ancient Egypt, we do find numbers of mighty pharaohs well known to history–we need only mention Ramesses II the Great, Akhenaten (the heretic). Then coming forward in time we have the Berber Hannibal Barca of Carthage, whose daring threatened Rome. In the case of both Egypt and Carthage, we had civilizations that had mastered the art of writing, and they dealt with Greece and Rome, which had long since done the same. In Africa, with her millions of people down through the centuries, we are left without written records. This had the effect of not only stifling external knowledge of the remarkable African peoples, but also of inhibiting the development of African education and literary achievement. This is one of the great tragedies in world history. Since the introduction of formal education, following the arrival of Christian missionaries who came after the European colonizing powers, we see the wonderful achievements of African writers and poets.

The modern period, which followed the spread of self-government in Africa, produced respected leading political figures such as Nelson Mandela, Kwame Nkrumah, and

Julius Nyerere; in the field of literature, there is Chinua Achebe and many others. Yet, it can be fairly said that Africa's day is barely dawning.

But all of this leaves us contemplating a huge void . . . where are the results of these millions of lives over the many centuries; where are the great achievements of the present day? After all, independence for most African States came about only sixty years ago. What is wrong?

The answer to that question is this: *what is wrong is a failure to achieve the proper recognition of human dignity on a multi-national scale.* This failure has directly led to the production an almost universally bad government on the continent of Africa. There exists corruption, contempt for law, lack of due process (on the part of governments), and contempt for the collective citizenry of its many countries–for their rightful entitlements and for their very lives.

How did all of this start going wrong? What has been brought down and left weighing heavily upon Africans, this curse of damaged or even denied human dignity? It can be argued that it started with slavery perpetuated through its history, while elsewhere around the world it had ceased largely to be a factor.

Now, it is true that every society in the world can find slavery in its origins. We have mostly been told the American story, that slavery was something done exclusively to African people by Europeans. This is a salve to American liberal consciences–they may feel good clutching that guilt–but it is not the truth. Slavery was practiced in every ancient people's history, and the slaves were usually their conquered enemies. Their fate was either death, absorption into the conquering army, or being kept or sold as slaves. It did not matter where they came from. Their skin color did not matter. Slavery was about victory–slaves were part of the victor's *loot*.

This was as true within Africa as everywhere else. We know this because when Mohammedanism was invented in the A.D. 600s, it began its warlike attacks around the Mediterranean. It destroyed some one-hundred-sixty Catholic Dioceses in North Africa. By way of trans-Saharan camel, trains began trading with West African Tribes. The trade swiftly extended to slaves, which the West African chiefs held and were keen to sell. This trans-Saharan slave trade went on for some 900 years. The Mohammedans simultaneously opened sea-borne slave trade with East African chiefs.

So it happened that Africa became stalled in its attitudes toward human dignity. Slavery was more important to the chiefs. Indeed, we could reasonably say that it was the existence of, and domination by the chiefs that strangled the development of the concept of human dignity.

Woe piled upon woe when, in the 1500s, the Europeans arrived by sea in West Africa, and the chiefs immediately saw the prospect of a bigger market and higher prices from slavers serving the sugar plantations of Cuba and the cotton plantations of the United States. This trade continued until the 1830s on the part of England (use of ships), 1865 in the United States, and 1886 in Cuba. By this time, Africa was gripped by another inhibiting factor in the progress of human dignity–colonial administrations.

The Colonization of Africa

Africa had experienced invasion and colonization in the distant past–concentrated in North Africa. We think of the Greek presence in Egypt from around 700 B.C., then the Roman conquest of Egypt, followed by the Vandals who descended on North Africa out of France and Spain. They established a Kingdom which lasted from A.D. 434 to A.D. 534.

However, for our purposes, it is the later European colonization which provides the relevant interest. It began with the Portuguese, whose Henry the Navigator commenced exploratory voyages in the late 1400s. In 1488, another Portuguese named Bartholomew Diaz had reached the Cape of Good Hope. European exploration in this period did not so much lead to colonization as to the establishment of trading posts. All the while, the Mohammedan slave traders were spreading their networks throughout inland Africa. In 1830, France gained a colonial foothold in Africa with the conquest of Algeria. The motivation behind colonization was mixed. Certainly, it was heavily influenced by the potential for trade. From time to time, it was also strategic, and, on occasion, a moral element was added to the mix. This might seem strange since we now see the very business of colonization as being immoral: akin to theft of sovereignty, but other factors were also at work. Consider this statement by the French statesman, republican, active Freemason, and enemy of the Church, Jules Ferry as late as 1884: "The higher races have a right over the lower races, they have a *duty to civilize the inferior races.*"[1] We do not have to guess who the *higher races* were in his view. The French took this duty seriously at the theoretical level. Colonials could aspire to French citizenship, and it was common to hear it insisted that they were French. However, there was always a degree of hypocrisy about this claim, for colonials were always treated as subjects rather than equal citizens.

The United Kingdom itself was a composition of conquest and colonization. England had conquered Scotland, Wales, and Ireland. Often, this was accomplished with bloody force and cruel oppression–particularly in Ireland. England sent settlers who dispossessed the Irish of their

---

[1] Jules François Camille Ferry, "Speech Before the French Chamber of Deputies, March 28, 1884," Discours et Opinions de Jules Ferry, ed. Paul Robiquet (Paris: Armand Colin & Cie., 1897), 1-5, 199-201, 210-11, 215-18. Translated by Ruth Kleinman in Brooklyn College Core Four Sourcebook.

Chapter 10: Africa: Human Dignity at Risk

lands, forced them into cruel tenant status, banned their Catholic religion, and even exported their food for profit. This despite the fact that throughout the several famines resulting from failures of the potato crops which were the staple food of the impoverished Irish. In effect, the Irish people were made peasants in their own land.

It was not surprising then that the United Kingdom was the leading colonizer in the world, supported by her massive and long victorious Royal Navy. However, Africa presented problems which made her relatively unattractive to the United Kingdom. Far distant Asia was rich in spices, exotic plants, and could be reached by more easily navigated routes. These routes provided constant and predictable winds, thus making them preferable. At the other extreme–at the end of the Earth–the United Kingdom was able to dump her own poor, as well as the troublesome Irish convicts. They were taken to remote and geographically inhospitable Botany Bay in the Great South Land of the Holy Spirit, which was to become Australia.

But Africa, virtually on her doorstep, presented nothing but problems. There were no favorable prevailing winds. In fact, there was the deadly phenomenon of the Doldrums off her West coast. The relatively accessible Mediterranean coast of Africa was under the control of the hostile and corrupt Mohammedan Ottoman Empire. Within Africa, there seemed to be nothing but problems. They knew of a multiplicity of fearsome and deadly diseases against which

Europeans had no natural defenses and certainly no medical cures. Further, the vast continent was teeming with peoples, many of whom had rather sophisticated systems of native rule and were capable of mounting a defense of their territory which would make it costly to colonize. To sum up, it was thought that the *game was not worth the candle*, so to speak. There was no need, no apparent opportunity, to justify getting involved. Or so it was until 1688.

In that year, a Protestant Dutch Monarch replaced the deposed Catholic King James II at the invitation of the British Government. This abrupt Anglo-Dutch alliance radically changed the United Kingdom's view of Africa. It introduced the United Kingdom to superior Dutch banking, corporation law, and concepts of a stronger Parliament. Now, for the first time, British and Dutch traders were able to work collaboratively instead of as competitors. In 1698, an Act of Parliament was passed which freely gave licenses to any trader to Africa for a 10% fee. This fee covered the first thirteen years of their trading activity. After that, there was no tax at all. No one could guess at the time that in the coming decades the full force of the industrial revolution would make use of this facility in a grand fashion.

But before this developed, the individual traders had caught on to the slave trade. The Dutch had been vigorous in developing the slave trade through the Dutch West India Company, which started in 1660 out of trading posts which spread progressively in what are now Ghana, Benin, Togo, and Nigeria. For a time, the company, along with the British, French, Portuguese, and Danish, operated slave trading posts in Ouidah in the Kingdom of Whydah in the South of what is now Benin. The trade was organized and facilitated by the Kingdom of Whydah. The region became known as the Slave Coast. By the 1690s, the United Kingdom had surpassed the Dutch as leaders in the trans-Atlantic slave trade. The Dutch operated in the trade until 1760.

Not only slaves were traded, but also ivory, palm oil, and clothing. Of all the colonizing European nations, perhaps none was worse than Belgium, which colonized the Congo. This was an extraordinary exercise in several ways. First, the territory of the Congo was seventy-six times larger than Belgium itself. Second, it was originally not possessed by the Belgian Nation, but was the personal property of the King of Belgium. This was the result of a disagreement between the King and the government of Belgium. The government was wary of colonial involvements, particularly in Africa with all its disadvantages of disease, huge populations, and access. However, the King was willful and, without the support of the government, proceeded to use his royal status to form an association with some English entrepreneurs. They set up the Congo Free State in 1885. The administration of this private enterprise was an appalling scandal. They developed trade in exporting rubber and ivory. In the process, their treatment of the Congolese people was extremely harsh, even barbaric at times, and the Congolese proved vulnerable to European diseases, especially Smallpox. There is no certainty, but there are estimates that millions of Congolese died from these diseases. In time, the barbarity of the treatment of the Congolese became a scandal throughout Europe. Pressure on the Belgian government grew so strong that it finally moved to take control of the Colony in 1908. The name was changed to the Belgian Congo. It remained true that the Belgian Congo was highly segregated, with privilege accorded to the European population.

German colonization in Africa has a much longer history and was more extensive. It began in the 1680s when the Margrave of Brandenburg (later to become Prussia) took possession of two small settlements on the Gold Coast, in what is today Ghana. By 1884, Germany's influence had grown so much that the Berlin Conference was held to decide on the carve-up of Africa by the contesting colonial powers. German colonies in Guinea and modern Nigeria's Ondo State failed within a year. Colonies in Cameroon, Namibia, Tanzania, and Togo quickly became successful. However, the defeat of Germany in World War I led to the League of Nations' distributing control of these substantial holdings between Belgium, France, Portugal, South Africa, and the United Kingdom. This was the end of the German colonization of Africa.

The Danish colonization of Africa began in 1658 as a result of the acquisition of the former Swedish colony in what is today southeast Ghana. It was acquired by the Danish West India Company, but in 1750 was taken over by the Kingdom of Denmark as a Crown colony. In 1850, it was sold to the United Kingdom.

This brief survey of the European colonization of Africa cannot do justice to the subject. However, it does serve to give some idea of the extent and variety of the experiences involved. In its inception, colonization always involved intrusion by trade or by force, if necessary. It was founded on the presumption of superiority–not only of education and development, but most often the belief of innate superiority of race. At its best, it was usually patronizing; at its worst, it was cruel and uncaring. It seems true to say that most of the colonizers regarded the peoples of Africa as inferior in every respect. The exceptional African, who managed to acquire an education and succeed brilliantly, was viewed as something of a freak of nature. The colonization by the Belgians was, by far, the worst; the Danes and the Germans were somewhat better. The French colonization left a distinct cultural and administrative character in their former colonies. As it has been around the world, the British approach to colonization seems to have worked the best for most of those colonized. Firstly, their habit of indirect rule through existing or established Chiefs of the people seems to have preserved a greater sense of self-respect among the peoples. The administrative apparatus they set up also served well as a model for locals to adopt, as did the system of British Law and education at all levels. As a result, former British colonies have, by and large, succeeded better than most other former colonies. Some, however, have certainly not achieved their potential. Some elements in former British colonies maintain an inordinate hatred of all things British, except their football (soccer) teams, which seems to far exceed all justification.

Our primary concern is human dignity. How was human dignity affected by the experience of the European colonization of Africa? One would have to say that it was assaulted sometimes in the worst possible way. We are not talking about slavery, which pre-existed European settlement by at least two-thousand years. Nor are we talking about subjection, for Africans were already familiar with, and accustomed to, subjection to their local and regional tribal chiefs, their kings, and to those who might conquer their local chief or king. No, the adverse impact of European colonization lay in this: *it was an unwelcome intrusion usually achieved through use of force–often by lethal force (the ultimate attack on human dignity).* Adding insult to injury, *the justification for this intrusion was predicated on the belief in the innate superiority of the colonizer over the colonized.* This degradation of the human African person was continually reinforced through intrusions and punishments.

Chapter 10: Africa: Human Dignity at Risk

One cannot help but wonder: in our present time, what would be the condition of the African peoples, their human dignity, had there been no European colonization? Certainly, there would have been millions more Africans alive–who would not have been killed by disease and by violence. We might also wonder: how would those deaths just mentioned compare to the number of deaths from starvation and native diseases that would result by not having European farming techniques and advanced medicines? At the less dramatic level, how many Africans today would choose living in the *state of nature* villages, their lives governed by custom, tradition, and superstition, over their present post-colonial lives in a modern society? The zealot will insist: *we would have been better left with the old ways, the traditions of our ancestors.* This is not conjecture. One can read them saying just that on social media. It is plain, however, that the great masses of African people have no desire at all to choose the former.

Truth is that this is all idle speculation. Colonization happened. Independence followed in the immediate post World War II period. If human dignity is to mean anything, it must be achieved in the here and now. The past is just that . . . *past*.

Tribalism

Africa is the home of many different tribes. The people of Africa rely on their tribal origin as their principal source of identification and relationship. One might belong to a country, but what gives him his sense of identity and belonging is his tribe. The origins of the tribe lie in the family and then the clan, and the tribe is the final development–the source of identity and of pride. All tribes have governments. Among the vast throng of tribes are these:

- The Afar tribe, which inhabits the horn of Africa in Ethiopia, Djibouti, Eritrea, and Somalia. They were grouped into kingdoms and rule by the Sultan of each group.
- Still, in Ethiopia, we find the dominant group of the area is the Amahara.
- Moving down to the Republic of Ghana, we find the Anlo-Ewe people.
- Also, in the Republic of Ghana, we find the renowned Ashanti tribes which often go by the name Asante.
- The Berbers are the indigenous inhabitants of North Africa and can be traced back to 3000 BC. These people can also be seen across Algeria, Morocco, Tunisia, Libya, and Egypt.

- The Dinka people who live in the Bahr el Ghazal region of the Nile basin, Jonglei, Southern Kordofan, and the Upper Nile region, is another major tribe.
- The Fang people live in forest clearings of the humid rainforests of Gabon. They are perhaps best known for the guardian figures which they attached to wooden boxes holding their ancestor's bones.
- The Masai once occupied large areas of East Africa. They are known as great warriors and herders.
- The Pygmies are known for their small size; they live in central and western Africa. There are many pygmy tribes including the Bambuti, Bayaka, Batwa, and the Bagyeli.
- The San is an African tribe are also referred to as Bushmen, Barwa, Sho, Kung, or Khwe. They live in the Kalahari desert and are the oldest inhabitants of South Africa. They were traditionally hunters and gathers but in modern days have become farmers.
- The Tutsi tribe is also referred to as the Watutsi. In Rwanda and Burundi, they are the 2nd largest caste.
- The largest caste is the Hutu and the smallest is the Twa Zulu. They are the largest ethnic group in South Africa, numbering about 10 million. Most of the Zulu live in the province of KwaZulu-Natal. They are renowned as warriors and famous for the

exploits of their leader Shaka Zulu against British rule.[2]

Tribalism gives a sense of pride in the mind of every African, and it is the skeletal support of African society as a whole. One's tribe adds importance and identity to him and precedes his citizenship of any country. For instance, a member of the Igbo tribe is proud of being an Igbo man, more so than generally identifying himself as a Nigerian. The idea of tribal belonging, rather than the national identity, is a special feature of African society though not necessarily unique.

Having seen this loyalty of the African man towards his tribe, one can better understand the nature of every African. With the arrival of the Europeans came the introduction of the concept of nationalism, which was superimposed on all African tribes. This was done without regard for the existence of tribal governance arrangements. Since the idea of the love of one's tribe remained, and yet remains strongly in the minds of every African man, there existed some inter-tribal disputes and wars pertaining to where each tribe started and ended in terms of boundaries and common rights of the tribes. It was hard for most African tribes to adapt to a national system of governance.

---

[2] Africa Facts, "People of Africa," https://interesting-africa-facts.com/Africa-People/Africa-People.html, Accessed 2018.

Since nationalism has been introduced into the system of government, and tribes merged to develop new national families, it is important to stop aggressive attitudes towards other tribes in each nation. This will be necessary in order to further the development of the society in which man now lives. When those in power focus on the betterment of the tribes they came from, to the exclusion of the interests of the nation, they impoverish the members of other tribes, leading to violence and poverty. This is an offense against human dignity. Also,

> "The difficulties of these new times demand a new vision and a renewed courage to transform our society and achieve justice for all. We must fight for the dual goals of racial and economic justice with determination and creativity. There must be no turning back along the road of justice, not sighing for bygone times of privilege, no nostalgia for simple solutions from another age. For we are the children of the age to come, when the first shall be last and the last shall be first, when blessed are they who serve Christ the Lord in all His brothers and sisters, especially those who are poor and suffer injustice."[3]

---

[3] U.S. Catholic Bishops, *Brothers and Sisters to Us*, (Washington DC: USCCB, 1979).

Africans need to represent their tribes in the government for the growth of the African states at large. Do not forget: *Ubuntu ungamntu ngabanye abantu* (translation: A person depends on other persons to be a person).

Life

In Africa, the respect accorded to life cannot be appreciated without a clear look at the notion of personhood in the African setting. Personhood is an attribution based on the way one acts in society, conforming to the rules and norms of society as a standard of judgment. Alternatively, it might be said that personhood is only recognized if one conforms. It is the recognition that the society accords, not the reality of personhood, which is a gift of God. This idea of personhood in the African setting is not something which all inherits from birth. Rather, it is believed to be what society allows one to be. One can be attributed to the good in his personhood when he acts in the ways that conform to the demands of society, be it in regard to religion, culture, or many other things. For instance, among the Igbo people of Nigeria, there is a designation of the human person through their native Igbo language that has personhood attributed as *Mmadu*. The *mmaduness* in the human person is what gives him his respect in society, but it also implies the possibility of the denial of such respect. On the other hand, one can act in a way that contradicts the norms of society by disregarding the social, religious, and cultural trends which one is expected to follow. Personhood, in the African setting, can be said to be actualized when one conforms to the dos and don'ts of the particular society in which one lives. It is also necessary that, in order to live a good life which defines one's personality, there must be an idea of the whole or *ubuntu* in one. It is the idea of recognition of the other; the act of belonging to a group. In Africa, though we came to be individually from birth, there is instilled in us the idea of the whole, so as to enable us to live a good life and define our personality in a positive manner. It is living as a group that defines Africans. One cannot boast of being an African without first being proud of the group to which he belongs. For instance, when asked who I am, I will never hesitate or be ashamed of mentioning that I am an Igbo man. It completes the identity of an African and adds value and respect to his personality.

Having looked at the nature of the personhood of man in African society, it is the right time to look at the value of life by these Africans. The Africans value life as a gift from God, as indicated in the previous chapters. Man's coming into the world serves as a mystery, and his life is also a miracle to him and to others. It is on this note that the Africans see life as a precious gift that we have no power to terminate.

For Africans, life is a divine gift which ought to be protected by any means necessary. The Africans can go the extra mile in protecting their lives from any danger that may deny them this precious gift from God. It is to honor this precious gift that they have special days set aside to thank God Almighty, which the Igbos of Nigeria call *Chukwu Okike*, for the gift of *Ndu* (life). There are also special days for reparation and restitution. On such days, many sacrifices are offered in reparation for their sins, for the elongation and betterment of life. Each day there is always a prayer said by the head of every family for the protection of life and for the guidance of the entire family. During this time, certain rituals are performed in order to call upon the family's ancestors, asking them to help and witnesses to our petitions.

In the African traditional religion, each man, upon his death, is not said to have entirely lost his life, nor is death seen as the termination of life. Rather, it is seen as a period for the renewal of the life of man and a means of judging the nature of the life lived in the society. At this moment, man is seen as descending into the spirit world, *Ala Mmuo* in Igbo, where reincarnation or, alternatively, punishment is determined. At death in the traditional African society, there are certain rituals that ought to be done, depending on the type of life lived, of which the entire members of that society are the witnesses. If it has been a good life, one is sent to the spirit world. There, he is reincarnated and sent again into society, after which, one of his physical features may be seen on someone from his generation, and he is believed to reincarnated, which leads to another ritual. In this ritual, he is welcomed into the family, where such persons can be revered as an ancestor. At this point, libations can be poured in his name for the protection and guidance of the living.

On the other hand, when one lives a bad life, his spirit is sent out totally from the society in which he lived. This sending is accomplished through certain rituals that are designed in such a way that the deceased cannot frighten or harm the living. He is then punished in the spirit-world and can never again be called an ancestor, for he will never be welcomed into that particular group of family ancestors. This, because he lacked certain qualities in his life, qualities that deny him certain rituals during his journey to the spirit world.

These aforementioned good qualities should be seen in all living African men, especially with respect to the life of others. Unfortunately, in the present world, those qualities are sadly lacking. A loss of calmness is seen in him. He is now seen as a *wolf* to his fellow Africans. The great continent has become an arena for the execution of various wicked acts. These acts show contempt for the idea of a better life. This is a consequence of the civilization that was introduced into Africa, which displaced traditional, social, and cultural values. To those who remain close-minded to current facts of life in Africa, this introduction of foreign culture brought nothing but tears instead of joy. Yet, to those open to self-development, it did bring joy along with, education, health, and knowledge of a wide world of personal and communal improvement. The different approaches can be seen in the family of the great Igbo writer, Chinua Achebe. His grandfather never embraced Christianity. He clung to the *old ways*. His father, however, became an Anglican and participated fully in the life of the Anglican religion and brought Chinua up as a modern educated young man, whose career was a brilliant success. Chinua had romantic respect for his grandfather's approach but lived his life fully and happily as a man who, without losing his Igbo identity, could move at ease in any society.

Racism in Africa

Racism is a term widely used in the modern world. It is a pejorative term describing the identification of a person by his race, doing so for the purposes of treating him badly. This may be through segregation, which results in the limitation of activity, opportunities, or rights.

There have been, currently are, and probably will be, attempts by many politically motivated persons to mobilize the power of the societal revulsion toward true racism. These people attempt to describe all manner of expressions, events, things, processes, etc. as being forms of *racism*. This crude and cynical effort is often well-received by the mass

Chapter 10: Africa: Human Dignity at Risk

media, so-called *progressives*, Marxist academics and their sycophants. This tactic suits the purposes of all of them and utilizes at least two of Socialist Saul Alinsky's *Rules for Radicals*.[4] The mainstream media are not interested in truth, but in sensation and controversy, which sells and produces income. For the Marxist academic, the same sensation and controversy help to push their radical agenda for the demolition of the present society and its Christian foundations.

According to the USCCB, "Crude and blatant expression of racist sentiment, though they occasionally exist, are today considered bad form. Yet racism itself persists in covert ways. Under the guise of other motives, it is manifest in the tendency to stereotype and marginalize whole segments of the population whose presence is perceived as a threat. It is manifest also in the indifference that replaces open hatred. Many times, the new face of racism is the computer print-out, the graph of profits and losses, the pink slip, the nameless statistic. Today's racism flourishes in the triumph of private concern over public responsibility, individual success over social commitment, and personal fulfillment over authentic compassion."[5] This

---

[4] Bolen Report, https://bolenreport.com/saul-alinskys-12-rules-radicals/, accessed March 30, 2020.

[5] U.S. Catholic Bishops, *Brothers and* Sisters *to Us*.

is typical of the left-wing social commentary found in many of the documents from the same source.

The racist character dominating the African continent came first from the tribes, seen in their attitudes to one another. That this is so is amply borne out in the most horrific fashion, by the genocidal warfare between the Hutu and the Tutsi in Rwanda. In a few months in 1994, the Hutu majority slaughtered between 500,000 and 1,000,000 Tutsi while the world stood aghast at the horror unfolding in the most appalling butchery of a proud and noble people. The distinct racial differences among the various tribes, from the very tall swaying Swahili to the diminutive Pygmy peoples, from the aggressive Zulu warrior class to the genial Kalahari Bushmen, could be utilized to justify and enflame racism.

The colonizers and the westerners brought their own racist tendencies to Africa, generally seeing all of the indigenous peoples as being inferior. They also took note of the racial differences between tribes and were quite adept playing one tribe off against another; using them to facilitate their colonial rule.

When the colonialists merged the different African tribes, the sole aim being to unite them into the various new nation-states, they compounded the problems. African tribes had already developed the idea that each tribe is unique and special. It cannot be compared with any other tribe. Merging these tribes frustrated relationships already

Chapter 10: Africa: Human Dignity at Risk

historically tense; relationships that existed when the tribes were independent. Tussles ensued revolving around such tribal matters as: Whose traditions and cultures should be followed, and whose should be abandoned? Which political system was to be employed in the government, so as to carry everyone along in that society?

For instance, since I came from the Igbo tribe of Nigeria, I see it as the best identity I have. When mixed with other tribes, I still see my own tribe as possessing the best socio-political and cultural system, thus making it superior to any other. Therefore, every other tribe, apart from my Igbo tribe, is inferior. Furthermore, the other tribe should be thrilled to adopt the organized system of my tribe. The same thing can be said of the colonialists, when Africa was seen as a land of no growth, a land inhabited by an uneducated population, and a continent seen as inferior in all respects. This is made clear through the famous term, *the dark continent*,[6] coined by British explorer Henry M. Stanley in the year 1878. This term accurately expresses the views of western colonizers toward the lands and peoples of Africa. This racist attitude toward Africans made it possible for the westerners to proceed to govern, with almost complete disregard, the peoples of Africa, their customs, their societies, and/or their wishes.

---

[6] H. M. Stanley, *Through The Dark Continent* (London :Sampson Low, Marston, Searle and Rivington, 1878), 47-48.

The same racist behavior can still be seen in the relationship that exists between those of African descent and those of the European descent. In some countries, the Africans are seen as people not worthy to reside in a particular geographical area. As a result, they are often segregated in the marketplaces, organizations, schools, buses, and in many other places. Their color became a factor that calls for segregation on them. The same thing is applicable to the Irish, who see the presence of the Africans in Ireland, where they constitute 1.4% of the population, as a discomforting one. Some portion of the African women with children are sometimes said to be publicly abused. In the United Kingdom, they constitute 3% of the population, double that in some cities. This density of African population can exacerbate potential racial stresses.

For centuries, many Africans living both within and outside of African societies (in diasporas) were faced with racism and segregation. This caused poor education, unemployment, and resultant poverty in these areas. The lack of a normal healthy interchange of ideas and interests between Africa and the rest of the world diminished the opportunities for the development of African countries and peoples. According to Saint Pope John Paul II, "We should add here that in today's world there are many other forms of poverty. For are there not certain privations or deprivations which deserve this name? The denial or the limitation of human rights as, for example, the right to religious freedom, the right to share in the building of society, the freedom to organize and to form unions, or to take initiatives in economic matters–do these not impoverish the human person as much as, if not more than, the deprivation of material goods? Is the development which does not take into account the full affirmation of these rights really development on the human level?"[7]

Thanks to the World Conference Against Racism, Racial Discrimination, Xenophobia and Related Intolerance, which was held in the year 2001,[8] an effort was undertaken to eliminate racism towards people of African descent, which also served as a means of emphasizing that Africans are also human persons. *Defeating racism, tribalism, tolerance, and all forms of discrimination will liberate us all, victim and perpetrator alike* (Ban Ki-moon). This has helped in creating awareness of African descent, and the inherent worth of Africans as humans created in the image and likeness of God. Africans are now associating with several countries of the world, despite the fact that they are still sometimes segregated in certain places more

---

[7] Pope John Paul II, "Solicitudo Rei Socialis," trans. Joseph G. Donders, *John Paul II: The Encyclicals in Everyday Language*, (Maryknoll, Orbis Books, 2001), §15.

[8] World Conference against Racism, Racial Discrimination, Xenophobia and Related Intolerance, (Durban, 21 May to 1 June, 2001), §31.

than in the past. The fact still remains that racism will disappear from legal texts only when it dies in people's hearts. However, there must also be direct action in the legislative field. Wherever discriminatory laws still exist, the citizens who are aware of the perversity of this ideology must assume rise to the moral challenge. By doing so, the democratic processes can produce legislation that is in harmony with the moral law. Within all states, the law must be equal for all citizens without distinction. A dominant group, whether numerically in the majority or minority, can never do as it likes when it comes to the basic rights of other groups. It is important for ethnic, linguistic, or religious minorities who live within the borders of the same state to enjoy the recognition of the same inalienable rights as other citizens, including the right to live together according to their specific cultural and religious characteristics. Their choice to be integrated into the surrounding culture must be a free one.[9] What is expected from the African continent is to stand out against social exclusion by putting more effort into the education of the little ones and youths, to help raise more voices from Africa against racism so as to create the common association that ought to exist among continents. Such efforts will, in turn, be better for

---

[9] The Pontifical Commission on Justice and Peace, *The Church and Racism: Towards a More Fraternal Society*, (Vatican City: Libreria Editrice Vaticana, 1988), §29.

Chapter 10: Africa: Human Dignity at Risk

our continent. After all, "no one is born hating another person because of color of his skin, or his background or his religion. People learn to hate, and if they can learn to hate, they can be taught to love, for love comes more naturally to the heart than its opposite,"[10] according to Dr. Martin Luther King, Jr. Additionally, a pastoral letter from the Black bishops in the United States reads in part as follows:

> "We must encourage Black leaders in the American Church–clergy, religious and lay. Unhappily, we must acknowledge that the major hindrance to the full development of Black leadership within the Church is still racism. Blacks and other minorities are meagerly represented on the decision-making level. Inner-city schools are disappearing, and Black vocational recruitment lacks support. This subtle racism still festers within our Church as it does in society. Some progress has been made, but much remains to do. This stain of racism, which is so alien to the Spirit of Christ, is an opportunity to work for renewal through evangelization... The causes of justice and social concern are an essential part of evangelization. To preach to the powerful without denouncing oppression

---

[10] Nelson Mandela, *Long Walk to Freedom: The Autobiography of Nelson Mandela*, (U.S.A. Little Brown & Co, 1994).

is to trivialize the Gospel. As Black people, we must have concern for those who hunger and thirst for justice throughout the world. We must not ignore those whom others tend to forget and even contribute our efforts and money. When we share our talents and our possessions with the forgotten ones of this world, we share Christ. This is the essence of evangelization itself."[11]

Therefore, let us continue with this awareness on the value and inherent dignity in the people of African descent because we are also human, for, as Dr. Martin Luther King, Jr., stated so eloquently, "I [we] have a dream that my four little children [the four parts of Africa] will one day live in a nation where they will not be judged by the color of their skin but by the content of their character."[12]

---

[11] A Pastoral Letter on Evangelization from the Black Bishops of the United States *What We Have Seen and Heard*, (Washington D.C, USCCB, 1984), Part II.

[12] Martin Luther King, Jr. speech at Civil Rights March (Washington D.C. 1963), BrainyQuote.com, BrainyMedia Inc, 2020. https://www.brainyquote.com/quotes/martin_luther_king_jr_115056, accessed March 20, 2020.

Chapter 11

Man with Dignity and the Society

The structure of every society is the product of the interaction of individuals, of which the society was composed, over a period of time. Perhaps paradoxically, that societal structure directly impacts the nature of the individuals living within that society. In turn, the nature of each man affects the society in a dynamic, but mostly imperceptible, process. For in society, man exists as an individual who started his development in the primary group composing the society, i.e., the family. As each grew, they ventured out to mingle with others. The concepts one forms concerning others outside the family are important, as one develops his association with others. The knowledge of one's own dignity, and the appreciation of the dignity of others in society, depends on the original teaching within the family about others.

In this appreciation of the dignity of others, combined with choices in the processes of the division of labor, man begins to establish the nature and extent of his contribution to society. The words of Pope Benedict XVI are, as usual, truly appropriate. He writes, "On this earth, there is room for everyone: here the entire human family must find the resources to live with dignity, through the help of nature itself God's gift to his children and through hard work and creativity. At the same time, we must recognize our grave duty to hand the earth on to future generations in such a condition that they too can worthily inhabit it and continue to cultivate it."[1] The family then serves as a loving preparatory class for every individual on how to face, and be received, in society. The common association in society begins as a group. It is here that one first puts into practice what he has learned within the family. He begins to pay attention to what is required of him within the group.

Association leads to the division of labor for the betterment of the common good of the group, to keep it going and alive. It makes each member realize the importance of the other. For instance, in a firm or organization, division of labor tells each individual what the firm requires of him for each day, leading to the health and growth of the firm. Here the union of the individual man and the society begins.

Man makes the society and, in turn, society makes man. This aspect of the oneness or bond that exists between man and society makes the actualization and recognition of

---

[1] Benedict XVI, *Caritas in Veritate*, §50.

human dignity most important. When man properly creates society, forming different institutions, norms, and rules to govern it, then society should be naturally inclined to help persons living within that society to achieve and flourish in their human dignity. Obviously, it ought never to be a way of exploiting man or a way of violating man's human dignity.

This chapter proposes a healthy society in which man lives with dignity. According to Pope Francis, "The dignity of the human person and the common good rank higher than the comfort of those who refuse to renounce their privileges. When these values are threatened, a prophetic voice must be raised."[2] For every man to be conscious of this inherent worth there needs to be a healthy society that will aid the actualization of this ideal. The promotion of human dignity must go beyond mere recognition of it, to actual respect for it in the human person.

The development of man with his due dignity is the aim of a society in which the socio-cultural systems are intended for the betterment of each and every individual. In *Rerum Novarum*, Pope Leo XIII taught that this kind of society can produce men whose dignities are recognized and realized. He writes,

---

[2] Francis, Evangelii Gaudium, §218.

"Now a State chiefly prospers and thrives through moral rule, well-regulated family life, respect for religion and justice, the moderation and fair imposing of public taxes, the progress of the arts and of trade, the abundant yield of the land–through everything, in fact, which makes the citizens better and happier. Hereby, then, it lies in the power of a ruler to benefit every class in the State, and amongst the rest to promote to the utmost the interests of the poor; and this in virtue of his office, and without being open to suspicion of undue interference–since it is the province of the commonwealth to serve the common good."[3]

Here, all institutions in society exist to aid man in the realization of his or her dignity. The mythologies, beliefs, and religion of the environment do not stand against the humanity of each individual rather, for the actualization of the common goal of the society which has its being in the Natural Law. For instance, there are certain primitive societies that have created myths that all individuals of the society emanated from a river. Therefore, every year there must be a human sacrifice to appease the marine spirits for the gift of life. There may be an agreement that virgins should be sacrificed to the water spirit every year in appreciation or atonement. Such superstitions attack the dignity

---

[3] Leo XIII, Rerum *Novarum*, 32.

of man. They are totally contrary to Christian teaching, of course. Even aside from considerations of true religion, we see man being used as a means to an end, not the end in itself. Even the philosopher Immanuel Kant stated, "Act so that you treat humanity, whether in your own person or in that of another, always as an end and never as a means only."[4]

A society is made habitable for all when there are sanctions for the effective maintenance of peace and decorum which stand against all deviant or aggressive behavior in society. This rule of law helps to eradicate totally the operation of the idea of *man's inhumanity to his fellow man,* the practice of which makes society a ground for combat. When one deviates from the laws of society and stands as a wolf to his fellow man, there must be measures that enforce what conscience ought to have obliged. Once everyone respects the rules and the norms governing their society which are enacted for the common good, respect for, and the realization of, the other's dignity is assured.

Society cannot promote the dignity of the human person when all are living in social isolation. Man was created in and for love. Though the dignity in each and every one of us is unique in itself, love, nevertheless, binds us together.

---

[4] Immanuel Kant, *Foundations of* the *Metaphysics of Morals,* trans. L. W. Beck, (New York: Library of Liberal Arts, 1959), 428–429.

For the fact that man is created by one Infinite Being. God is, as Saint John tells us, Love. In his own image and likeness, He establishes a common association among these specially created beings, for *no man is an island*. The dependent nature of man in society requires the recognition of the same status in all other human beings. Everything in the world exists in groups, and it was this that awakened the inquisitiveness of the pre-Socratic philosophers towards the multiplication of things in the world. It is the common interaction that exists in a group that makes it one and defines it. Therefore, the recognition and respect of the rights and dignity of others is achieved if, and only if, one is in the same place with them. Equally, one's dignity can never be recognized and promoted when isolated from others. The possession of reason and willpower by man makes him the controller of his actions, and thus responsible for them, whether they are right or wrong. The existence of rationality and the power to make choices are essential attributes of the dignity of man. Saint Thomas Aquinas (1225-1274), drawing on the Book of Genesis, further refined our understanding of the human person being created in God's image by interpreting Genesis to teach that the human person is an "intelligent being endowed with free will and self-movement."[5] Also, according to the *Catechism of the Catholic Church*, "Freedom is

---

[5] Aquinas, ST, I–II, Prologue.

exercised in relationships between human beings. Every human person, created in the image of God, has the natural right to be recognized as a free and responsible being. All owe to each other this duty of respect. The right to the exercise of freedom, especially in moral and religious matters, is an inalienable requirement of the dignity of the human person. This right must be recognized and protected by civil authority within the limits of the common good and public order."[6] It manifests the uniqueness of the individual person and only in a society, where man is allowed to exercise his free will, knowing that when he makes choices he has control over his life.

Society must provide for the dignity of every human member if it is to have any claim to integrity. In the political sector, all must partake in the government of society, and no one must be seen as either a minority or superior. The social class existing in society dehumanizes some and deprives them of their political rights: to vote, and to be voted for in an election. When one is excluded from the social group to which he rightly belongs, he is dehumanized and his dignity goes unrecognized. In a right-minded society, there should be no place for unnatural discrimination based on sex. Rather, all should be recognized equally. Such a society facilitates love according to the mind of the Creator of mankind. In every sector, it is obligatory

---

[6] *CCC*, §1738.

that all are eligible, consistent with nature, for any office or position in society.

The idea of war upon and destruction of the human environment and means of survival, is the most serious threat to such a society. For one can no longer be what he freely wills when there exists a state of war. War, of its very nature, involves threats to the respect of the other's worth and value. In war, we neglect and violate human life; the precious and fundamental gift given to man, from which all other rights originate.

This ideal society must have its focus on the common good of all mankind, ranging from those in public office to the last man in that society. Society is not for selfish desires. Thus, it should endeavor to give to each man his rightful due. It was in this light that Saint Pope John XXIII solicited for a better society when he said,

> "A sane view of the common good must be present and operative in men invested with public authority. They must take account of all those social conditions which favor the full development of humanity. Moreover, We consider it altogether vital that the numerous intermediary bodies and corporate enterprises–which are, so to say, the main vehicle of this social growth, be really autonomous, and loyally collaborate in pursuit of their own specific interests and those of the common good. For these groups must themselves necessarily present

Chapter 11: Man with Dignity and the Society

the form and substance of a true community, and this will only be the case if they treat their individual members as human persons and encourage them to take an active part in the ordering of their lives."⁷

Therefore, it will be an ideal step if we make a change in our various societies to be able to emerge fully as humans with dignity, not *servants* to be excluded from the environment in which we were asked to dominate.

"Once more, however, we must emphasize the need of laying a sure foundation in the individual mind and conscience. Upon the integrity of each, his personal observance of justice and charity, depend the efficacy of legislation and of all endeavors for the common good. Our aim, therefore, should be, not to multiply laws and restrictions, but to develop such a spirit as will enable us to live in harmony under the simplest possible form, and only the necessary amount, of external regulation. Democracy understood as self-government implies that the people as a whole shall rule themselves."⁸

---

⁷ John XXIII, *Mater et Magistra*, §65.

⁸ Catholic Church in the United States, Pastoral Letter of the Archbishops and Bishops of the United States Assembled in Conference at the Catholic University of America, September,

For the best way to fulfill one's obligations of justice and love is to contribute to the common good according to one's means and the needs of others. Also, to promote and help public and private organizations devoted to bettering the conditions of life.[9]

1919, (Washington, D.C.: The National Catholic Welfare Council, 1919), 71–77.

[9] John Paul II, *Gaudium et* Spes, §30.

Chapter 12

Conclusion

Harsh behaviors between individuals have disfigured societies in which man is not only the subject, but also the director and governor. As we know, society is the product of a community of men in a given region. Such society exhibits all characteristics of men themselves: it can flourish, grow, wither, and die.

Through his actions, man not only transforms both things and societies, but also tends to perfect himself.[1] He not only affects society, but is also affected by it, whether the action is positive or negative.

Africa is a large continent of vast societies with a rich diversity of human and animal occupants, as well as resources, varied landscapes, rivers, lakes, and mountains. In this work, we have studied the abuse of man by his fellow men–even to the point of dehumanization–principally in Africa. Still, there may be other continents worse

---

[1] Ibid., §35–36.

off. It is perverse for man's rationality to be used to degrade his fellow man. Thus, society ought to be free ground for every individual to flourish—created, as he is, in the image and likeness of God and given his charter to subdue the earth and all the creatures in it–in justice and holiness.[2] Human selfishness and egotistical behavior have no place in this Divine Plan.

The lamentations of the oppressed and deprived in African societies call for the restoration of God-given freedom. Their loss of humanity at the hands of perverse men demonstrates the potential for stupidity in man and has unbalanced the African continent leading directly to an absence of peace and harmony.

In Africa, the quest for power, position, and prestige has deformed these societies and resulted in effective segregations and class structures. The Sacredness of each life and the essential unity of man are lost while human dignity, fraternal community, and liberty have disappeared as love has been driven out of the spirit of these societies. All the excellent fruits of nature and of our liberties, which would have multiplied on earth according to the mind of the Lord, will be re-discovered very late[3] if we continue act without love.

---

[2] Ibid., §33–34.
[3] Ibid., §39.

Chapter 12: Conclusion

In order for the restoration of liberty and freedom in African societies, and for the de-humanized and marginalized to regain their status as full members of society, elites must become aware that each person is a gift to every other person. As was said previously, no man is an island. Togetherness creates beauty. While each of us is a little star, together we illumine the world.

The association of men within a well-ordered society can create a synergy that leads to developments even greater than those achieved by individual members of that society. More can be achieved together–for good or for ill. However, this is only fully realized when every man develops himself and his potential fully, as God intended. In this way, we establish the solidarity, the true glory of man flourishing.

We can have a positive or negative effect on others. When we recognize the human qualities of each and every person within our society, both the person and the society will flourish. If we inhibit the expression of those human qualities, both the person and the society will be diminished.

Africa needs *we-power*, which is essential to every society, both the developed and the developing. This contrasts with the attitude expressed in the *I–Thou* formula. It is an ancient philosophical issue whose implicit concentration on "I" tends to undermine the love which God intends us to exhibit in our dealings with one another.

There is an adage amongst the Igbo tribe of Nigeria: "Igwe bu ike. We are powerful when we are together." We can do *impossible* things when we attempt them with, and for, one another. Our differences and realities, when within moral boundaries, beautify the society.

Individual talents distinguish man. Free to use these talents, he satisfies himself and, directly or indirectly, satisfies his fellows. Thus, each man can enhance his humanity and that of his fellows. Coming together with our talents, great and small, enriches our society and the world. Mankind is the product of the Divine Being, who has his Presence within man. Realizing this Divine indwelling in our relationships with others is our vocation here on Earth. The image of God in us should be expressed through our love of our fellows. As St. Irenaeus tells us, "For the glory of God, is a living man; and the life of man consists in beholding God."[4] We cannot validly seek liberty in human society without linking it to the Divine Will. Negation of the divine projection degrades and dehumanizes man and denies his proper nature.

This work has reviewed all the degradations, miseries, and intolerable oppressions that afflict many African societies, even in the modern era. At this time, there is a

---

[4] Irenaeus of Lyons, *Against Heresies*, Book 4, Chapter 20, §5-7 (Third Millennium Media L.L.C., The Faith Database L.L.C., 2008).

radical reformation, proceeding at a greater or lesser pace, of these evils to ensure justice for all African societies. This movement will assist Africa to take their equal place among the global community of nations. However, this must be attained without falling into the trap of Marxist subversion–the producer of intellectual and civil oppression. Africa will find freedom in the Truth of Jesus Christ, whose *Truth will make you free*.

This process will kick-start with the elimination of discriminating language, emphasis on skin color, tribal origins, etc. This will require a truly radical change of personal, as well as communal, attitudes. In the economic sphere, there must be an end to seeking prestige, privilege, and wealth for their own sake–without providing those same opportunities for the people. The mass media has its role to play through. It must forsake its concentration on distraction and shallowness. It must duly relate and praise real achievement; it must encourage constructive activity, praise hard work, and promote authentic education.

In the cultural sector of African societies, the law has a large part to play. The maxim is that everyone has *equality before the law*. This must apply to the laws themselves, as well as their application and operation. How humiliating it is that, in Africa, reputable international financial publications correctly and justifiably publish lists of African financial criminals and their offshore wealth–even ranking them. These criminals are at large, and still in positions of power in Africa. She must put her house in order before the maxim can become a reality in our continent. No one is born a slave or inferior. All are created in the image and likeness of God, having the decisive power that makes it possible to choose to help bring about the flourishing of their fellow man, as well as themselves.

Many types of conflicts scourge African societies. Some are traditional; some are of a more recent origin. Some are internal, some are particular to individual countries, and others are between countries. Often, we hear cries for the *West* to intervene, but any such action would be equally reviled as a *new colonialism*. We recall with horror the Hutu–Tutsi terrors, which led to the world looking on in disbelief–shaking its collective head at the reality that such inhumanity could occur. Even her African neighbors stood aghast. These are not easy problems to address, but it seems clear that the solution must be found among the African peoples themselves.

According to the Second Vatican Council, peace is not only the absence of war–it is the fruit of an order written in human society by its Divine founder, to be realized by men who aspire always to a more perfect justice. In order for peace to be obtained on Earth, it is a must that the good of the people be safeguarded; it must be that men communicate spontaneously, in truth, the richness of their minds and the will of their Creator. The firm will of each nation's rulers must be inclined toward respect for other men

Chapter 12: Conclusion

(including the nations in which they dwell) as well as their own dignity. The ardent and effective search for fraternity among all mankind is absolutely necessary for the construction of peace.[5] The fight of man against his fellow man is a fight against himself, for we are one and came from one Source, which is Love (God). In his comment on love, St. Augustine said: "he that hates another, does hurt his own soul."[6]

The hallmark of conflict resolution in Africa–as everywhere else–must remain *justice*. This applies at the individual, communal, and national levels. Without Justice, there can be no Peace. As Saint Augustine put it: "Behold Justice: behold Truth."[7] This thought moved Saint Pope Paul VI to say, "If you want Peace, work for Justice."[8] And as we extend Justice and bring Peace we will see diminish-

---

[5] Paul VI, *Gaudium et Spes*, §78-82.

[6] Saint Augustine, Sermons on the New Testament (Sermon 32),§3. Translated by R.G. MacMullen. From Nicene and Post-Nicene Fathers, First Series, Vol. 6. Edited by Philip Schaff. (Buffalo, NY: Christian Literature Publishing Co., 1888.) Revised and edited for New Advent by Kevin Knight. http://www.newadvent.org/fathers/160332.htm.

[7] Saint Augustine, *On the Psalms*, 95, 14-15. (Turnhout: Brepols Publishing, original edition 1956, second edition 1990), Latina Series, 1351-1353.

[8] Pope Paul VI, *If you want peace, work for Justice* (Vatican City: Liberia Editrice Vaticana, 1972), §1.

ing, the very idea of Africa as the *dark continent* of past European fears.

Religion is the true means by which Africa can be brought to this happy situation. However, it must be authentic religion–born of God–not the quackery, not the money-raking business that too often passes for *religion* in much of Africa.

The societies of Africa must embrace and practice religion founded on a love that sees man as being made in the image and likeness of a Good and Loving God; a religion that respects life and human dignity. Thus, these societies will re-awaken the sense of love and solidarity in African men and help in the restoration of the authentic sense of the connection to the Divine.

Religion should play a vital role in society by unifying its various sectors in principles, thoughts, and actions. Society must see and accept religion as a very important aspect of the life of man. This because through it, man connects with his Creator and thus his existence can be properly understood. When man respects and takes very seriously the ordinances of religion, it will go a long way to help the ordering of his conscience and directing him back to God who is Love. The recognition of the dignity of others, resting on the foundation of the Love which is God, may then be present in all sectors of society.

Authentic religious groups should carry out movements of peace, love, and liberation in African societies. By doing this, hope can be given to the marginalized, the dehumanized, the enslaved, the sick, and the maltreated in African society. These groups should teach and exemplify the equality of all men before God the Creator–the fraternity which shows that we are one and of One Source. The Order of the Most Holy Trinity and of the captives, a Catholic Religious Order founded by Saint John of Matha, dedicated to the works of charity, hospitality, liberation, and the ransoming of captives, is known worldwide for its works of mercy and liberation in society, for the betterment of humanity and the greater glory of the Most Holy Trinity. This is an exemplary instance of the kind of movement required in African societies, though it is certainly not the only Order in the Church similarly engaged. As viewed by Saint Peter Chrysologus, the Creator looked for what to add to our dignity: he gave us his *image and likeness* so that our visible image on earth might reflect the activity and will of the Creator among men.[9]

Through works of love, man sees the image of God in his fellow man. God is Love, and we were created in his image and likeness, that is to say, this resemblance of God. The Holy Spirit dwells in the inner heart of man, which is chiefly in our souls, as the *Catechism of the Catholic Church* teaches. However, it is through the body that this love is

---

[9] St. Peter Chrysologus, "Homily on the Mystery of the Incarnation," ii 148. *Latin Patrology*, 596–598.

expressed into the visible world. As Venerable Fulton Sheen tells us, "The plan of the Incarnation [*of taking for himself a human body*] was based upon the communication of the Divine through the human, the invisible through the visible, and the eternal through the temporal. It was, in a certain sense, the foundation of a Sacramental universe in which material things would be used as the channels for the spiritual."[10] Therefore, it is not enough to simply *feel* love in your hearts. The African man can, and must, be dignified through the *act* of loving others in the society, For love conquers and covers all, and among all we do in our societies today, "love is the greatest of them all." (1 Cor. 13:13)

---

[10] Archbishop Fulton J. Sheen, *The Mystical Body of Christ*, Ave Maria Press, Kindle Edition, 26.

www.ingramcontent.com/pod-product-compliance
Lightning Source LLC
Chambersburg PA
CBHW071158160426
43196CB00011B/2122